CROSS-CULTURAL COMMUNICATION

Perspectives in Theory and Practice

Thomas L. Warren

Baywood's Technical Communications Series
Series Editor: CHARLES H. SIDES

Baywood Publishing Company, Inc.
AMITYVILLE, NEW YORK

Baywood Publishing Company, Inc.
P.O. Box 337
26 Austin Avenue
Amityville, NY 11701
(800) 638-7819
E-mail: baywood@baywood.com
Web site: baywood.com

Library of Congress Catalog Number: 2005046539
ISBN: 0-89503-318-6 (cloth)

Library of Congress Cataloging-in-Publication Data

Warren, Thomas L.
    Cross-cultural communication: perspectives in theory and practice / Thomas L. Warren.
        p. cm. -- (Baywood's technical communications series)
    Includes bibliographical references and index.
    ISBN 0-89503-318-6 (cloth)
        1. Intercultural communication. 2. Documentation. I. Title. II. Series.

    P94.6.C763 2005
    302.2--dc22

                                                                2005046539

Contents

Contents

Preface

This collection of essays represents the past few years of my work in cross-cultural communication. I first became interested in cross-cultural communication in a serious way in the spring of 1989 when, as an assistant to the president of the Society for Technical Communication (STC), I was at a board meeting and heard a call from Janice Hocker, the president, for the report of the INTECOM delegate. When none appeared, she raised the issue of continuing STC's membership in that organization, even though STC was a founding member.

I was sitting next to Dick Wiegand and asked him what that was all about. He told me that the STC delegate to INTECOM, an international organization of technical communication organizations, had not attended a meeting or filed a report for some years and that the board was considering dropping its membership. I told him that I would take on the job (not having the faintest idea what it involved), and Dick proposed me as the new delegate. I was given one year to produce some sort of results.

So, in October 1989, my wife and I headed to England (our first stop) and then on to Copenhagen for the INTECOM meeting. What I found was a small, highly dedicated group of delegates committed to improving technical communication on a worldwide scale by assembling once a year in a member nation for a two- to three-day meeting where issues relating to technical communication were discussed. Many of the INTECOM meetings were held in conjunction with the host's annual conference, so INTECOM delegates participated by giving papers and being on panels.

One constant theme from then until I no longer represented STC at INTECOM was culture and the role culture plays in communication. Another frequent topic was how INTECOM works and benefits its members. I took that opportunity to begin researching cross-cultural communication and the impact it would have on transferring information from one culture to another. I was also able to offer some classes on the topic at Oklahoma State University in our Technical Writing Program. Finally, my contacts with other society delegates through INTECOM got me invitations to present papers on cross-cultural communication at their conferences.

This book represents a number of aspects of cross-cultural communication, beginning with how quality (a term just as evasive to define as is *culture*) relates to communication across cultures. In terms of date of composition and presentation in print form (all but one has appeared in print form), these essays (Chapters 2 to 6) represent a chronological organization, starting with the essay on quality and culture and ending with a recent paper presented at the tekom (German technical communication society) conference.

My main focus throughout the essays is to address ways that technical communicators in small- to medium-size companies could make their documents more acceptable when they crossed cultural borders. There are a lot of resources available for translating and localizing documents, but smaller companies frequently do not have the financial resources to take advantage of them, placing the burden on the author. Technical communicators who produce documents in these smaller companies have so much to do that the audience analysis phase of preparing the documents is superficial at best. If they can become aware of techniques and strategies that they can apply as they are creating the documents, then they can, I think, generate documents that are more acceptable.

Acknowledgments

I would not have been able to develop this area of research had not
Dick Wiegand believed—as did Janice Hocker—that I could effectively bring STC representation to INTECOM. I also appreciate the
many, many conversations I had with delegates—past and present—
to INTECOM and with the many conference audiences who listened
to and challenged my ideas. Charles Sides, as editor of the *Journal of
Technical Writing and Communication*, published several of these
essays and encouraged me to develop them into a book for Baywood
Publishing Company. There have also been reviewers of both the
essays and this book manuscript, and I am grateful for their time
and assistance. And, of course, my wife, best friend, and strongest
supporter, Mary Lee, made sure that I kept both feet firmly on the
ground when developing the conference presentations that became
the essays and this book.

CHAPTER 1

Introduction

Transferring information across cultures has often presented difficult and complex communication problems. For example, avoiding cultural mistakes that would prevent or modify the communication has frequently occupied technical communicators, especially because of the international character of their documents, not to mention their importance and the recently enacted guidelines for documentation (in the European Union, for example). Advances in translation and attention to localization have gone a long way to improving these communications. But such translation services are expensive, and many small- to medium-size companies cannot easily afford such costs yet want to participate in the worldwide market. Likewise, the advances in localization come at a financial cost that these companies also cannot afford. And a new problem is beginning to appear: outsourcing of jobs, particularly jobs related to technical translation and localization, and while the costs for both are reduced, many times the quality is lower. One set of problems emerging with outsourcing relate to cultural differences between the author and the reader, magnified by adding another culture to the process.[1] One solution is to analyze the recipients of the information better, especially their

---

[1] What I am commenting on here is sending translation/localization work offshore—to, for example, India. When a German company wants its documents translated into English for use by Americans and it sends the job to India, another culture is added to the mix. There is now the German culture originating the documents, the Indian culture translating and possibly localizing, and the American culture of the reader.

culture, and to develop writing strategies that help enhance the value and acceptance of the information.

Technical communicators typically analyze their audiences, focusing on such elements as demographics, the audience's role and responsibilities within an organization, and the psychological/cognitive need for the information [1]. Communicators are also concerned about where the user will use the information (sitting comfortably in a chair or on an off-shore oil rig); the user's attitude to the whole process (including the attitude toward the subject, the communicator, and the genre); and a myriad of other issues. Realistically, when communicators must produce information in a form and format that the product or service requires, they face a series of strict deadlines so that when the need for audience analysis arrives, they have had very little time to do a thorough analysis. Some large companies establish predetermined audience analyses for their product and service documentation in an effort to produce uniform documents [2]. Smaller companies, however, rely on the communicators to be well-trained in audience analysis and to perform it, when appropriate, as they develop their documents.

My concern in these essays is not translation (although some of the advice could prove useful when preparing documents for translation and localization). Rather, my concern is with the technical communicator who prepares documents in American English for users whose first language is not American English. In instances like these, the communicator faces two problems.

1. Does the communicator rely exclusively on a limited vocabulary for the documents (such as one of the many forms of Basic English)?
2. How much time is available to do a cultural analysis of the users and then adapt the text accordingly?

The first problem involves one or more of the many forms of Basic English (also called Simplified English). Basic English may work well for documents that will be translated (or at least localized), saving considerable time and money in the translating costs, but such an approach often leaves the document devoid of nuances, depth or richness, or style, or all three. In addition, many communicators are unfamiliar with the linguistic, semantic, and syntactic requirements imposed by Basic English [3].

The second problem is more acute. The communicator must determine the cultural context for the document and construct or adapt a document that not only will be acceptable to the users but will also demonstrate cultural sensitivity. Such a process involves understanding just what *culture* is. One definition [4] sees some cultural elements as being made manifest in the objective characteristics of a society: codified rules, regulations, and laws of the society's legal, moral, ethical, and religious systems. Other cultural elements are identified through the subjective codes: interpretations of the objective elements as well as rules, regulations, and laws of a society that are not codified in their legal, moral, ethical, and religious systems. The first set of codes is readily available for those wanting to learn about any given culture. The Bibliography at the end of this book is full of such resources. The subjective codes, however, are not as readily available, so that the communicator must infer them. Both learning efforts are time-consuming and, especially in the case of the subjective systems, prone to misinterpretation. However, this approach to defining *culture* is relatively simplistic. Another approach that often works is to think about the cultural elements as being those elements that guide people through their daily lives [5]. These include such things as language and gestures, philosophy and values, courtship and marriage, food, work, education, health care, and various systems such as governmental and communication. The definitions provided in dictionaries use these approaches [6-9]. The approach I prefer to use in this book is the one I mentioned above: the objective and subjective elements of the cultural group [4].

OBJECTIVE ELEMENTS
IN CULTURE

Objective elements in a culture include such things as the rules and regulations that govern the people and are codified in the various laws (city, county, state, federal). For example, most countries have speed limits for their highways. In addition, religious cultures have codified the expected behaviors of the people accepting that religion, and these are available in the sacred books and commentaries. For example, most religious cultures prohibit killing another person. Language is another kind of culturally objective element. It typically has grammars, dictionaries, and style manuals that codify the language.

These laws and regulations are constantly evolving in the legalistic, legislative, and religious parts of the culture through regulatory bodies as well as secular courts where offenses against the civil laws are tried and ecclesiastical courts where violations of religious codes are prosecuted. In short, these objective elements are quite visible, and the technical communicator needs to be aware of them when writing documents. While the objective elements are visible, the subjective ones usually are not.

SUBJECTIVE ELEMENTS
IN CULTURE

The subjective elements are much more difficult to identify and to locate. These include such things as a culture's values, norms, beliefs, and attitudes. (For early research on the subjective elements of a culture, see Hofstede [10-12].) In the example of speed limits, what is the attitude of the drivers toward speed limits? Do they try to evade the law? In the United States, several companies make radar detectors that are popular and, though illegal in some states, sell extremely well. Laws have other subjective sides based on how judges and law enforcement officers interpret them—the circumstances when speeding is permitted. In most religions, you can identify conservative, moderate, and liberal interpretations of the objective codes. These tend to be orally transmitted or inferred from pronouncements of the religious leaders. Killing another person may be justified, for example, in a war. In language you also have subjective elements in the connotative meaning of words. There are also disagreements about permissiveness relating to grammar, usage, and spelling. Again, the acceptance of these positions is usually inferred.

Further complicating the issues is a traditional versus a modern interpretation of situations. For example, we frequently generalize about the "traditional" Eastern attitude toward some aspect of the culture. Time is a good example. McGrath's anthology [13] has several essays that examine time in a cultural context, comparing actual attitudes to "traditional" attitudes concerning time. This and many similar issues are causing problems when in conflict with the more "traditional" view. In the case of time, are the people of Japan abandoning their traditional view about time in favor of a more Western view? Robert Levine's essay on the pace of life [in 13] shows that the Japanese involved in the study tend toward a more Western approach to the pace of life—much faster than the traditional view.

Because such interpretations are seldom written down but are intuitively known by the members of the group, technical communicators writing documents for use in these cultures have a difficult job. Communicators certainly do not want to offend their users by committing a cultural gaffe in their documents. Consequently, they localize their documents or at least have some sort of review before distributing them. This approach is reactive. What I am suggesting is a proactive approach when developing the document.

The difficulties arise when communicators confuse the subjective elements of a culture with the objective elements. They can more easily identify the objective "rules" that govern a culture (such as the religious, linguistic, and legal laws published for all to know), and consequently will often rely completely on them. Knowing the more subjective elements of a culture (elements that are not codified in sets of "rules" or "laws") can help communicators prepare documents that users will more willingly accept. For example, what is the cultural attitude toward time (linear or circular? a river or a pool?); business communications (get the message up front fast or establish a relationship between writer and reader before getting to business?); the individual—my example below—(an independent person seeking personal success or a person seeking to have the group rather than the individual succeed?).

Certainly, it is difficult for the communicator to prepare documents for native English speakers that have all the quality characteristics normally associated with professionally prepared materials without having to consider various cultural issues. Yet, the global economy demands that the materials cross cultures.

The kinds of problems and the subsequent embarrassments are well known [14, pp. 370-371], and the sources in the Bibliography show that a lot of people have been concerned about this problem and have offered multiple suggestions in many disciplines and from many perspectives. Nancy Hoft's 1995 book [15] has proven invaluable for communicators wanting to make their documents more acceptable to cross-cultural audiences. Especially useful are her worksheets that help the technical communicator analyze the culture of the user. Even textbooks in technical report writing are now including a section or a whole chapter on communicating across cultures, offering advice for students on how to be aware of what they say and the cultural impact it will have. For example, two approaches used by textbooks are providing an individual chapter on cross-cultural communications and scattering material throughout, based on the topic the author discusses (see Table 1 for an overview of four current texts) [16-19].

Assuming that the future technical communicators will come through classes that use these textbooks, which method is best for learning to adapt text to different cultures? The answer is that all four textbooks do a good job on surface elements of text—things like audience analysis, colors, language (why *Nova* failed as a car name in South America, for example), and so forth. Should there be more in-depth coverage? Should the students be taught about things like cultural implications of metadiscourse, rhetorical strategies, communication theories, and the like? Perhaps. But my experience with students at this level suggests that the granularity of coverage offered by these four books is sufficient for their needs both in class and

Table 1. Four Current Texts' Coverage of
Cross-Cultural Communication

Author	Title	Pages	Coverage
Anderson [16]	*Technical Communication*	Scattered throughout	General observations about effect of culture on communication. No sustained discussion or specific guidelines.
Houp et al. [17]	*Reporting Technical Information*	Chapter 7, pp. 125-153	Explains influence of culture on communication. General suggestions for adapting text to different cultures.
Lannon [18]	*Technical Writing*	Scattered throughout	Suggestions based on genre and communication preparation. General recommendations about style, usage, and language.
Markel [19]	*Technical Communication*	Scattered; extended discussion of audience, pp. 87-96	General suggestions; does go beyond the surface analysis.

later on the job. Typically, they will work in their disciplines for companies that, if they did business across cultures, would make sure that the communications reflected the culture of the customers—or so we would hope. I doubt that these employees would be the ones who actually prepared the documents unless they would be correspondence, and the textbooks mentioned in Table 1 do a good job in that area. My attention in these essays moves beyond the more surface elements to consider ways a technical communicator can adapt text to different cultural contexts.

In looking to adjust and adapt text to different communication situations, technical communicators can address the fundamental areas of vocabulary, sentence and paragraph structure and organization, visuals, and a host of other aspects of the content when communicating within the culture. When communicating that content across cultures, the communicators must add another layer to this adaptation: the differences in culture. The Appendix (p. 109) summarizes a wide variety of issues in comparing a traditional Western culture and a traditional Eastern culture (note that I am using generalizations about the two cultures that are changing and require the technical communicator to narrow the cultural audience analysis). Based on cultural expectations, communicators can prepare effective documents for culturally diverse audiences. Understanding the context goes some way in understanding how to make the information more acceptable to users in different cultures. But is that enough?

CULTURAL ANALYSIS

Adapting text to different cultures involves many different textual aspects. Some of these are

1. Words—semantics
2. Metaphors
3. Paragraph structures
4. Syntax
5. Context

In addition to these items, there are others:

1. The reading habits of the people in that culture
2. The way people argue

3. Issues of old-new information (e.g., Williams [20]) as they apply in languages/cultures other than English.

Reading Habits

In Western cultures, people use different strategies for reading texts. For example, Pugh identifies skimming, scanning, and reading for detail as three of several strategies Western readers use [21]. Yet, what about non-Western readers? Do they approach a text in the same psychological way so that the communicator can provide frequent summaries (for skimming), informative headings (for scanning), and details (reading for details) for those in other cultures in the same way?

Argument

How do people argue in different cultures? Or do they? What constitutes evidence in different cultures as well? If someone says, "This is the case," this may work in some cultures if someone is vested with authority to speak on the subject (another culturally defined characteristic). How is credibility of the authorial voice established? Can the technical communicator assume that credibility comes from authorship per se? How are authors viewed in other cultures—ours as well as theirs?

Old-New Information

One interesting feature about style in Western cultures is the old-new information arrangement for sentences [20]. What are the cultural implications when analyzing a text for that old and new information from a different culture? To take a simple example, does placement of the predicate in German change the old-new information scheme? And what about languages that are not syntactic but rather inflected? This old-new issue introduces the further issue of context. Does context (pragmatics) in non-Western cultures work the same as it does in Western cultures? How do the readers in non-Western cultures understand context? Do authors rely much more heavily on the reader already understanding the context—both generally and specifically in reference, for example, to antecedents for pronouns? Western readers of imaginative literature (poetry especially) learn early on that they supply their own context to the work. And, it seems, many carry this model over when they use technical documents, and those who produce those documents often assume that the context is self-evident to the reader or supplied through the occasion of the reader coming to the document. Do readers in other cultures carry the same considerations for context?

Added to these difficulties are the issues that readers of English as a second or third language bring to documents. Can we assume that they change their concepts of reading patterns, argument, and old-new information schema from their native culture to the culture of the document?

These issues that I raise are certainly candidates for future research and guidelines/suggestions. I mention them here to give you a sense of the enormity of the problem facing technical communicators who have to transfer information across cultures. My concerns in these chapters are more modest.

ISSUES ADDRESSED IN THESE ESSAYS

When adapting text for different audiences, communicators can work with such linguistic features as semantics, metaphors, sentence and paragraph structures, syntax, and context. They also can reorganize sentences, paragraphs, and sections based on the old-new arrangements. Other elements that the communicator can work with are metadiscourse, language codes, and communication and rhetorical strategies. Chapters in this book focus on these later elements by looking at specific examples and analyzing them based on one or more of these features of text.

In Chapter 2 ("Issues in Internationalization of Technical Documentation: Quality Control") I look at matters relating to quality in documentation and cross-cultural communication. Technical communicators find quality control problems differ substantially when they write for readers whose first language is not their own because these problems extend beyond the quality of the translation. Those who write in English for native readers of English frequently identify quality with quantitative measures that are document- and reader-centered. Those writing for other readers (readers for whom English is not a first language) find that they must apply other measures as well, such as those associated with cultural differences. Communicators writing in English for readers whose first language is English develop a document within a framework of assumptions grounded in both research and experience that become questionable when the reader's first language is not English. The issues are beyond the question of translation and localization quality, and one cannot measure the quality of documents by traditional means.

In Chapter 3 ("National Cultures in International Communication") I look briefly at the cultural basis for language, including language codes. Then I look at a specific device authors can use to provide users with context (metadiscourse) and analyze an example. Because technical communication involves senders (authors), messages, and readers (users), relationships among these three elements are predicated on informational goals: for the user, the need for specific pieces of information; for the author, responding to that need for information. The author accommodates the reader in a number of ways by adapting the information so that the reader can understand it. For example, the author can use syntactical arrangement to communicate information about the information or provide additional wording to tell the user how to read the text. Among the many ways the author can communicate meaning is context (pragmatics)—both primary (the text, or direct experience, or both) and secondary (the cultural context). The user, if the language the message uses is the user's first language, should understand the cultural context. If the message's language is not in the user's first language, the author should not assume that the reader is familiar with the cultural context of the message. The author must carefully select appropriate language codes for not only the content but also the cultural implications. In short, the author has much to think about when preparing the message.

In Chapter 4 ("Communicating Style Rules to Editors of International Standards") I analyze ISO TC 184/SC4 style documents looking at how standards committees (specifically, one ISO standard technical committee) deal with consistency and quality in their draft standards. Prior to approval, these standards must pass through several reviews for technical accuracy and stylistic appropriateness. The style considerations are based on documents published by both the umbrella organization (International Organization for Standardization, or ISO) and the various committees and subcommittees within it. Because authors and editors who use these documents frequently do not have English as a first language, the documents must explain unambiguously just how committees should prepare their documents. This study looks at a sample of those instructional documents using Brustein's Restricted and Elaborated Codes and metadiscourse analysis to determine how easily users can read and understand the material. The findings suggest that the documents do not send a clear message to authors and editors and can be stylistically hard to understand. Consequently, the approved standards themselves are hard to read, interpret, and apply.

In Chapter 5 ("Cultural Influences on Technical Manuals") I look at how technical communicators produce manuals that may be less than effective because of cultural elements. This chapter discusses the cultural elements in developing a document and shows, through a comparison of two hypothetical cultures, how the document will differ when organized for those two cultures.

In Chapter 6 ("Increasing User Acceptance of Technical Information in Cross-Cultural Communication") I look at how technical communicators can apply different theories (communication and rhetorical) to improve the cultural acceptability of their documents. A significant problem in technical communication is persuading the user that the information is accurate, valid, and useful. All too often, technical communicators treat users as members of their own culture. When authors do consider cultural issues, they often focus on matters such as vocabulary, visuals, and organization. Other strategies, however, can be useful in gaining acceptance of technical information in cross-cultural situations. For example, the communication theory of *compliance-gaining* offers suggestions for how technical communicators can adapt the text to enhance user acceptance when communicating to members of their own culture as well as when communicating across cultures. In this chapter, I explain several compliance-gaining strategies authors can use, identify rhetorical strategies they can combine with compliance-gaining strategies, show how these strategies can be effective in a cross-cultural environment by comparing the strategies in two hypothetical cultures, and analyze a brief sample.

Chapter 7 is a general conclusion and a pointing ahead for future research projects. It also offers some guidelines for developing documents that can gain wider acceptance through awareness of cross-cultural as well as composing elements.

The book concludes with an extended Bibliography of works relating to cross-cultural communication. It should provide a starting point for future research into the many aspects of the subject.

REFERENCES

1. T. L. Warren, Three Approaches to Reader Analysis, *Technical Communication, 40*:1, pp. 81-88, 1993.
2. S. Schultz, F. Kavanagh, M. Morse, and J. Darrow, *The Digital Technical Documentation Handbook,* Digital Press, Burlington, Massachusetts, 1993.
3. See, for example, S. K. Shubert and others, The Comprehensibility of Simplified English in Procedures, *Journal of Technical Writing and Communication, 25*:4, pp. 347-369, 1995; also D. Eckert, The Use of Simplified English to Improve Task Comprehension for Non-Native English Speaking Aviation Maintenance Technician Students, *Dissertation Abstracts International, A: The Humanities and Social Sciences, DAI-A 58/12,* p. 4629, June 1998.
4. M. R. Limaye and D. A. Victor, Cross-Cultural Business Communication Research: State of the Art and Hypotheses for the 1990s, *The Journal of Business Communication, 28,* pp. 277-299, 1991.
5. F. Jandt, *Intercultural Communication: An Introduction* (2nd Edition), Sage Publications, Thousand Oaks, California, pp. 3-23, 1998.
6. J. Pearsall (ed.), *The Concise Oxford Dictionary* (10th Edition), Oxford University Press, New York, 1999.
7. A. H. Soukhanov (ed.), *The American Heritage Dictionary* (3rd Edition), Houghton Mifflin, Boston, 1992.
8. A. H. Soukhanov (ed.), *Encarta World English Dictionary,* St. Martin's Press, New York, 1999.
9. D. Thompson (ed.), *The Concise Oxford Dictionary of Current English* (9th Edition), Clarendon Press, Oxford, 1995.
10. G. Hofstede, *Cultures and Organizations: Software of the Mind,* McGraw-Hill Book Company, New York, 1991.
11. G. Hofstede, Cultural Predictors of National Negotiation Styles, in *Processes of International Negotiation,* F. Mautner-Markhof (ed.), Westview Press, Boulder, Colorado, pp. 193-201, 1989.
12. G. Hofstede, *Culture's Consequences: International Differences in Work-Related Values,* Sage, Beverly Hills, California, 1987.
13. J. E. McGrath (ed.), *The Social Psychology of Time: New Perspectives,* Newbury Park, California: Sage Publications, 1988. Contains James M. Jones, "Cultural Differences in Temporal Perspectives: Instrumental and Expressive Behaviors in Time"; Robert V. Levine, "The Pace of Life Across Cultures"; Rebecca Warner, "Rhythm in Social Interaction"; Janice R. Kelley, "Entrainment in Individual and Group Behavior"; Jonathan L. Freedman and Donald R. Edwards, "Time Pressure, Task Performance, and Enjoyment"; John P. Robinson, "Time-Diary Evidence About the Social Psychology of Everyday Life"; Richard L. Moreland and John M. Levine, "Group Dynamics Over Time: Development and Socialization of Small Groups"; Allan W. Wicker and Jeanne C. King, "Life Cycles of Behavior Settings"; Carol M. Werner, Lois M. Haggard,

Irwin Altman, and Diana Oxley, "Temporal Qualities of Rituals and Celebrations: A Comparison of Christmas Street and Zuni Shalako"; and Daniel Stokols, "Transformational Processes in People-Environment Relations."

14. K. A. Schriver, *Dynamics of Document Design,* John Wiley & Sons, New York, 1997.

15. N. L. Hoft, *International Technical Communication: How to Export High Technology,* John Wiley & Sons, New York, 1995.

16. P. V. Anderson, *Technical Communication: A Reader-Centered Approach* (5th Edition), Thompson/Heinle, Boston, 2003.

17. K. W. Houp and others, *Reporting Technical Information* (10th Edition), Oxford University Press, New York, 2002.

18. J. M. Lannon, *Technical Writing* (7th Edition), Longman, New York, 1997.

19. M. Markel, *Technical Communication* (7th Edition), Bedford/St. Martin's, Boston, 2004.

20. J. M. Williams, *Style: Ten Lessons in Clarity and Grace* (7th Edition), Longman, New York, 2003

21. A. K. Pugh, *Silent Reading: An Introduction to Its Study and Teaching,* Heinemann, London, 1978.

CHAPTER 2

Issues in Internationalization of Technical Documentation: Quality Control*

Quality is a term that has always been difficult to define. Do we consider it measurable or intangible? Hirst [1, p. 454] points out that in the history of Western thought, Robert Boyle (*The Origin of Forms and Qualities,* 1666) described a "quality" or a characteristic as being primary (measurable) and secondary (non-measurable). Locke, in his *Essay Concerning Human Understanding* (1690), gave the issue its classical formulation when he argued that material objects possess five measurable, primary qualities:

1. Extension (size)
2. Figure (shape)
3. Motion or rest
4. Number
5. Solidity (impenetrability)

They also possess several secondary, nonmeasurable qualities:

1. Color
2. Taste
3. Smell
4. Sound
5. Warmth or cold

*This chapter has been modified from Thomas Warren: Originally published as, Issues in Internationalisation: Quality Control pp. 171-184 in *Quality of Technical Documentation*. Edited by Michaël Steehouder, Carel Jansen, Pieter van der Poort and Ron Verheijen. Rodopi 1994. (Copyright © Editions Rodopi BV, Amsterdam/New York, NY 1994). Reproduced by permission.

Primary qualities (characteristics) of an object for both Boyle and Locke are inherently capable of being quantified. We can measure each to rather precise levels and can agree, using standard measuring instruments and techniques, on values found in objects. Secondary qualities (characteristics), however, are relative to the observer. What smells one way for me could smell another way for you and even though we can measure the odor, each individual must assess its quality regardless of the measurement (what we measure are the odor's primary qualities). Thus, it becomes extremely difficult to quantify them.

Engineers can, for example, quantify the primary characteristics of a transistor because it is a material object. They can also measure the primary characteristics (what I will later call the surface features) of a document because it, too, is a material object. But what of the characteristics of the design of the transistor and the document beyond those primary characteristics? Can we quantify something (design) that is not a material object? Is there something in design (of an object) that is beyond the reach of measuring devices?

Robert Pirsig [2, pp. 233-234] identifies quality with what is non-measurable: the moment when people have an experience is the moment they instinctively recognize that experience as possessing or not possessing quality. They seem to know intuitively that one experience contains quality while another does not. Pirsig also argues that when a number of people are exposed to the same experience, there can be some general agreement on the presence or absence of quality. Yet it is impossible to quantify these experiences so that one can infuse an experience with quality. When a person reads a document (or any written matter), can measurable characteristics determine the quality of that piece?

Turning to the dictionary fails to offer much more help on how to define *quality*. The *American Heritage Dictionary* [3], for example, tells us that quality is "An inherent or distinguishing characteristic; a property"; a "personal trait, especially a character trait" or an "[e]ssential character; nature." Again, trying to quantify something as obscure as a characteristic of a secondary quality (or even in some instances a primary characteristic) presents problems. Yet we need to define the term in some way because of its influence on what we, as technical communicators, do.

My focus, as the title of this chapter suggests, lies with quality as an issue in cross-cultural relationships formed through documentation. When a native language speaker writes for a native language reader, there are many problems associated with the communication, as we are aware; for example, reader analysis—who will read this text and how will the writer adapt it to help the reader understand? Will the reader know the terms as well as the concepts? And what does the reader already know and what does the reader need to know? But the problems of communicating across cultures are not present, because both writer and reader are of the same culture. Those problems introduce a new set of issues.

In this chapter I want to highlight some of the difficulties of developing documentation for cross-cultural situations, and look at the problems of measuring its quality. After an overview of measuring and establishing quality in technical communications, I present a brief review of reader analysis (often argued as the primary guarantee of the quality of a document). Next I present views on writing documentation across cultural boundaries and an example of how attitudes toward various cultural elements influence the writer. The point I hope to make is that by ignoring issues related to culture, measures of quality provide only a part of the picture.

MEASURING QUALITY

When a native language user writes for a nonnative language reader, the problems multiply. This situation even exists when the language basically is the same, such as an American writing for a U.K. reader. (Within a country, there can be similar problems of communicating between and among various cultures, but that is not the focus for this chapter.) The problems are even more troublesome for the writer when the reader uses a translation. When the American author writes for an American reader, we have traditionally been able to apply measures that presume to quantify quality.

Traditional Measures

Traditional ways of measuring quality rely on the surface features of a document, but they are document-centered rather than reader-centered. Writers can measure documents for three elements:

- *Readability* measures the surface features of a text such as number of syllables or three-syllable words, average sentence length, and the like. However, when writers apply readability measures to documents meant to communicate across cultures, they face difficulties because many of the inherent assumptions about language differ. Languages where long words and sentences are common may be easy to understand for one group but not another, even if the text is in English and the reader reads English as a second or third language: German readers, for example, are used to long words and sentences; American readers are used to short words and sentences. Hence, trying to measure the readability of a text written in English for German readers cannot successfully use these formulas.

- *Statistical analyses* count the numbers of passive voice verbs, prepositions, and the like and compare the results with standards for using each feature. For example, textbooks and other sources of advice on writing effective prose caution the writer about avoiding passive voice constructions and minimizing prepositional phrases. For a document written in English targeted to readers whose first language is not English, these elements may be considered positive rather than negative. Some languages depending heavily on structural modification (such as a prepositional phrase—as found in Dutch) would score poorly in such statistical analyses.
- *Usability testing* involves testing typical users with the documentation and quantifying the results against a standard. The difficulties associated with the artificiality of the test increase when you are testing across cultures. With testing within one culture, usability testing does have a rather artificial quality unless the testing occurs under the user's conditions rather than the tester's, and then there could be problems associated with how the observer influences the user.

These three are not the only traditional approaches to quality. Other traditional approaches to measuring quality rely on additional factors: accuracy, timeliness, and defects [4]:

- *Accuracy:* Is it accurate—as defined by the technical people who supplied the data that the writer used to develop it? This attitude is typical of the advice given to American documentation writers. Does it (can it?) apply to writers in other cultures as well as to readers in other cultures? The problem involves whether cultural accuracy is a primary or secondary quality—that is, is it a characteristic that we can measure or is it one that is intangible? The issue I raise here is one that questions whether or not we can measure the quality of a document that has been localized.

- *Timeliness:* Is it timely—arriving on the shipping dock on time? For cross-cultural communications, the writer would need to know how the user planned to use the documentation before deciding that timely delivery could be a criterion for quality (see below where I discuss how the reader uses documentation).
- *Defects:* Are there any defects in the document—such as spelling and grammatical errors? Problems here relate to problems of grammatical, lexical, and stylistic correctness as well as those problems found in translation and localization.

These measures relate to the reader only in indirect ways—they assume that, for example, certain features contribute to the document's understandability, and quality is present if the document is accurate, on time, and without defects.

With the preceding discussion as background, I turn now to the two new approaches to establishing quality in technical documents: managing the process and applying more sophisticated statistical analysis.

Managing the Process

Manufacturers, faced with conforming to quality standards (ISO 9000, for example), look to elements in manufacturing as quality control points. They have, historically, used quantifiable data to determine that quality. Each stage in producing a product is carefully evaluated for its contribution to the overall quality of the product.

In technical communications, it is rather hard to isolate and quantify the quality contribution of each stage in writing a document. One managerial response has been to make the technical communicator a part of developing a product from its conception through design and manufacture, where each stage adds value and some measurable form of quality to a product even if that product is a document. But the difficulty is that the human mind does not create ideas in a way that can be easily measured. The same is true with designing an object. So, in technical communication and product design, quality control focuses on the tangible document that has measurable (i.e., primary) qualities. Management, therefore, turns to things that it can quantify such as how long does it take to produce one page of text for any given document? Such raw measures ignore such important issues as the usability of the information. And that is where new statistical measures have evolved.

More Sophisticated Analyses

A combined effort by researchers from Rensselaer Polytechnic Institute, Carnegie-Mellon, NCR, and others has investigated the linguistic basis for quality that they believe will allow them to identify standards relating to such measures as clause structure, the statement's assertiveness, the rhetorical function of a statement (conclusion or not), and the kind of action it leads to. The standards also include percentages of noun strings, dependent clauses, independent clauses, conditional clauses, metadiscourse, and other countable measures [4].[1]

They base these standards on research into how people read. At issue is the question, does a user read differently than the casual reader? Regardless, these measures are a major step toward a standard that involves more than surface features. And yet, when you try to measure a document that crosses cultures, you find severe limitations and restrictions. Quality control, at least for documents meant for cross-cultural communication, offers challenges that looking only at the language cannot help.

A second significant area where technical communicators have sought to measure quality in a document is reader analysis.

READER ANALYSIS

Technical writers have known for years that they must understand who will read their documents if they want a document to communicate. Thus, various systems of analyzing one's reader have evolved [5]. Textbooks emphasize the need to analyze the audience before beginning to write or even plan. Writers typically analyze their audience so that they can match their language and style with the reader's, using any of several techniques to adjust the document to fit the abilities of the reader. For example, writers can offer such rhetorical modes as definitions, analogies, and descriptions; they may decrease the amount of text and increase the number of visuals;

---

[1] As of the date of this manuscript, little more has been done on this project. Yet, the concept does offer some possibilities when measuring text written in English for readers whose native language is English.

they can increase or decrease the complexity of those visuals; and they can vary surface features such as average sentence and paragraph structure and length. The effectiveness of these techniques relies heavily on readers and writers sharing a common communication environment and certainly introduces problems when measuring the quality of documents meant to communicate across cultures. When they do not share such an environment (in cross-cultural communications), problems arise not only with measuring quality but also with the more fundamental level of understanding.

What kind of reader analysis do writers perform when the writer is writing for a reader outside his or her culture? Is there time in the production cycle to consider all the cultural factors that the writer needs to consider? Or, rather, does the writer rely on generalizations about a particular reader's culture? For example, in an analysis of one reader group, Hein [6] determined that:

1. Readers wanted a lot of background information with strong organizational links found in overt statements.
2. They wanted a very large amount of data.
3. They would follow the instructions literally—word for word.
4. They held text in high respect, carefully inspecting it.

This profile describes a nation's readers.[2] In short, it is a stereotype. When writers rely on stereotypes, problems do not disappear—they multiply as they do with any overgeneralization. The level of detail when analyzing a reader of the same language as the writer also relies on generalizations, but not the sort that lead to stereotypes. For example, for writers preparing documents for readers within their own culture, Pearsall's approach to reader analysis [8] proves useful because it divides the general readership into five groups based on their jobs or why they need the information. Pearsall describes each group based on 13 characteristics. The result is that the writer has five generalized reader groups rather than one, and the five groups offer writers a means of narrowing writing choices when writing for an audience not personally known to them.

---

[2] Limaye and Victor [7] point out that cultures are not anchored to nations, so that one nation may have many cultures. The writer's problem is to develop approaches that will either cut across all cultures in a particular nation or develop documents meant for use by members of each culture. The latter, of course, is not practical, while the former is fraught with dangers in matters of more than language. See the discussion of cultural implications above and as shown in Table 1.

Table 1. Views of Time by Two Cultures

Linear view	Nonlinear view
Time is money	Time a natural event
Don't waste my time; I need to budget time	Time renewable, flexible
Be direct in approach	Be indirect in approach; direct seen as rude
Come to the point quickly	Communication is unhurried
Little introductory phrasing	No rush; set scene unhurriedly
Quick response expected	No rush; things happen when they do
Stay on the topic	Communication goes off on tangents
Efficiency measured against goals	Efficiency not a matter of time

Source: Adapted from Limaye and Victor [7].

If writers produce documents meant for another culture and want to use Pearsall's five reader groups, the categories could break down as could the five groups (because they were not meant to apply to readers in a different culture). Hence, this exact model would not work well, but the idea of identifying the readers and classifying them based on their organizational role and information needs could prove useful. But the assumptions implicit in Pearsall's model—that you can manipulate text based on the levels of formal education, the reader's role within an organization, and the reader's attitude toward the information—may easily lead the writer astray.

In 1994, a collection of papers presented at a conference on quality in documentation was published [9]. It contains a number of papers, including an earlier version of this chapter, that focus on quality in intercultural communication. Therefore, I have only summarized the problems writers face in determining the quality of documentation developed for readers within their own culture, pointing out the difficulties of communicating across cultures.

Before we can define quality standards for such documentation, we need to know what *culture* is—a term that almost defies definition (see my discussion of it in Chapter 1). For my purposes, however, and in keeping with the Boyle/Locke division of quality into primary and secondary, I want to follow Limaye and Victor's views [7] that culture has two distinct domains:

1. Objective domain—infrastructure and technology
2. Subjective domain—values, behavioral norms, religious attitudes

Just as we had *quality* defined in primary (measurable) and secondary (nonmeasurable) terms, so too is *culture* divided into objective (measurable) and subjective (nonmeasurable) domains. As with the secondary qualities, measuring subjective cultural elements proves illusive. The implications for the writer involve knowing both objective and subjective cultural elements and knowing how to adjust text to accommodate the reader.

It is easy to see problems that can arise with communication across quite different cultures: for example, from traditional Western to traditional Eastern cultures. There are major differences besides the language because there are also significant differences in the objective and subjective cultural domains. There can even be differences across similar cultures, but they are not, perhaps, as obvious: for example, when an American author writes for German readers. Language differences are not too great, nor are differences in attitude. But there are enough differences to make communication difficult.

If American technical communicators decide to measure quality in documentation meant for Japanese or German readers, what approaches should they take? Should they rely on the surface features alone? Can they factor in cultural elements? Or are they, finally, returned to Pirsig's view that you cannot measure quality because it is or is not present at that moment when a person has an experience and the person will know it intuitively—as will others? If that is true, then measures of quality both between and within cultures become academic exercises.

CULTURAL ISSUES

Cultural issues can parallel language ones. For example, do you address your reader directly? Or must you prepare the reader before launching into the actions? To some (Americans, for example), all instructions must be in the imperative verb mood. Even the information introducing instructions should be "you centered." But readers in some countries could consider second person too friendly and even condescending [10]. It could irritate the reader.

Another potential problem relates to the amount of context the reader wants. Developing a document for readers in a culture that wants large portions of the message unspecified and submitting the same document to readers in a culture that want a great deal of detail creates problems of understanding as well as quality. In addition, cultures that are used to a lot of detail emphasize rules more so than cultures that are used to low levels of detail [7]. That suggests not only a careful wording (second person, for example, rather than third) but also organizing documents where rules play a major role (software documentation, for example).

The overview (or summary or abstract) presents in condensed form the matters discussed in detail in the document. In reports, for example, the most read section by busy American readers is usually the summary.[3] Readers read the body only in order to find details supporting the writer's conclusions and recommendations, and then only in case they disagree with those conclusions and recommendations. Consequently, writers summarize the major points early in the document and readers read until satisfied that they have the information that they need. Americans need/want overviews and introductions, and their absence creates problems for the reader. Members of another culture may not need such apparatus, because they want to build a view of the document's subject slowly. These readers want to form their own views as to what is important, and they want to develop their own schema of the information rather than having the writer impose one.

The situation is similar for manuals. The American user probably reads enough about the command to execute it; "learning" comes through repetition of the command rather than cognitively comprehending it. In another culture, readers may read the entire document before reacting. So writers would have to use a different organizational approach entirely for the different culture (see Tables 4–8 in Chapter 3).

These problems are relatively simple and self-evident. Less so are problems related to cultural assumptions about such things as the concept of time, attitude toward self and others, the role of the

---

[3] For the details of the Westinghouse study that determined how American midlevel managers read reports, see Pearsall [8, p. xvi]. For details of a similar British study, see Turner [11, p. 68].

individual, views of work, and the like. Table 2 identifies 12 culturally determined factors and contrasts two hypothetical cultures—at the extremes—projecting implications writers must deal with when preparing any documentation for the two. Before turning to this table, however, I want to examine the concept of time as an example.

Cultures may view time differently. Table 1 shows how two cultures would consider time, with one culture viewing time as linear and the second viewing it as nonlinear. In trying to document a computer program for these two cultures, for example, the author faces a number of difficulties. In the view that time is linear and non-renewable, efficiency and short-cuts dominate, while they would be of little or no importance to one whose culture saw time as nonlinear and renewable. When deciding on whether such a manual had "quality" or met a quality standard, the evaluator would have to consider the two approaches as separate. In this case the issue facing the writer wanting to write a "quality" manual would be how to quantify the influence of the culture into the quality standard—that is, deciding which primary qualities to measure (and how) and evaluating the secondary qualities as to relevance.

With this difficulty of handling cultural concepts of time as an example, we can now turn to Table 2. (For more comparisons, see the Appendix, p. 109). The table presents extremes of two hypothetical cultures (represented by Views A and B) to demonstrate how wide differences can be. In practice, the differences could be less extreme because of the influence of global communications. In addition to showing extremes that may, in reality, be less severe, Table 2 suggests that one culture may be of one description for one feature (say, View A on time) and another on another issue (say, View B on the basis for one's actions). That, of course, is the difficulty of such a representation. By and large, though, there are interdependencies among the various topics and views. The place where you would likely find such a mixture of Views A and B would be within a multicultural country (the United States, for example). Writers face an even more complex challenge in circumstances such as these. As with most any reader analysis situation, you have to make the best evaluation and draw the most reasonable inferences about the reader. Ignoring the cultural elements, though, will lead to problems.

Table 2. Comparative Views of Two Cultures on Selected Cultural Topics

Topic/Issue	View A / View B	Implications of A / Implications of B
Perception of world; relationship to nature	A: One is separate from nature; master it B: One is part of nature; learn to move with it	A: Learning improves my control of the system B: I can become part of the system; Windows or Mac
Time	A: Stress future B: Stress present; living day-to-day	A: Need to learn to do task again, orientation in the future B: Need to know only what I need to know today
Perception of time	A: Time = river; moves quickly; keep up B: Time = pool; moves slowly; no rush	A: Quick reference materials; overviews; summaries B: Focus on details; no hurry; build picture slowly
Perception of others	A: Others are fragmented personalities; look at fragments B: Person is an entity; view other person as whole; accept or reject whole, not a part	A: Learning sharpens competition; further sets me apart B: Learning helps all; integrate into the system
Relations with community	A: All are equal B: Hierarchy; treat person according to position	A: Level playing field; documents designed for anyone doing the job B: Will learning change my position? Role and position of Help Desk
Resolving differences	A: Face-to-face B: Go through another; face-saving	A: Problems? Call guru, Help Desk; attack problems/people head-on B: Work to solve own problems; don't readily admit need for help

Perception of self and goals	A: Individual goals	A: "I want to do ..."
	B: Group goals	B: "We need to learn ..."
Views of activity	A: What a person *does* is important	A: Individual achievement; pay raises; become guru
	B: What a person *is* is important	B: Subsume to welfare of group; don't stand out
Work/play	A: Done at separate times	A: Clear separation of work and play; learning not a game
	B: Not separate	B: No time constraints needed to separate work from play
Basis for one's actions	A: Personal achievements; individual actions; free will	A: Learning helps me advance; focus on me
	B: Actions result from interpersonal relations	B: Improve organization; fate determines if whether I learn or not
Motivation	A: Competition	A: Learning gives me an edge
	B: No need to excel	B: Learning helps others; group benefits
One's actions; solving problems	A: Solve one's own	A: "... will let me do work."
	B: Depend on others	B: "... will make me a better worker"

Source: Adapted from J. P. Feig and L. C. Yaffee, *Adjusting to the U.S.A.*, Washington International Center of Meridian House International, Washington, D.C., no date.

CONCLUSION

Cultural diversity creates problems when you have to determine quality, because it involves much more than surface and countable primary features. Matters such as the perception of time, self, and community; motivations for actions and relations with others; and other elements are not easily translated into primary, measurable qualities. The difficulties faced by technical communicators who must develop and then conform to quality standards pose a challenge that is not easily met. The difficulties are much beyond those found in translation. Machine translations, for example, can achieve remarkably high levels of accuracy (a characteristic that one can quantify). More to the point, however, are those issues that stand at the back of language. The culture itself introduces views that emerge in language patterns. Using surface features never has been of much value in measuring the quality of documents. Even the new statistical analyses offer little or no help in measuring the quality of a document that ignores the influence of culture on how people read. The challenge facing technical communicators is to match the cultural assumptions of the writer with those of the reader.

REFERENCES

1. R. J. Hirst, Primary and Secondary Qualities, *Encyclopedia of Philosophy,* volume 6, P. Edwards (ed.), Macmillan Publishing Company, New York, pp. 454-457, 1969.
2. R. Pirsig, *Zen and the Art of Motorcycle Maintenance: An Inquiry into Values,* Bantam, New York, 1974.
3. A. H. Soukhanov (ed.), The *American Heritage Dictionary of the English Language* (3rd Edition), Houghton Mifflin, Boston, 1992.
4. W. J. Hosier and others, Basing Document Quality Standards on Research, in *1992 Proceedings,* 39th STC Annual Conference, Society for Technical Communication, Arlington, Virginia, pp. 428-431, 1993.
5. T. L. Warren, Three Approaches to Reader Analysis, *Technical Communication, 40*:1, pp. 81-88, 1993.
6. R. G. Hein, Culture and Communication, *Technical Communication, 38*:1, p. 125, 1991.
7. M. R. Limaye and D. A. Victor, Cross-Cultural Business Communication Research: State of the Art and Hypotheses for the 1990s, *Journal of Business Communication, 281,* pp. 277-1299, 1991.
8. T. E. Pearsall, Introduction, in *Audience Analysis for Technical Writing,* Glencoe Press, Beverly Hills, California, pp. ix-xxii, 1968.

9. M. Steehouder, C. Jansen, P. van der Poort, and R. Verheijen (eds.), *Quality in Technical Documentation,* Rodopi, Amsterdam/Atlanta, 1994.
10. S. Jones and others, *Developing International User Information,* Digital Press, Bedford, Massachusetts, 1992.
11. B. T. Turner, *Effective Technical Writing and Speaking,* Business Books Limited, London, 1974.

CHAPTER 3
National Cultures in International Communication

Technical communication involves senders, messages, and receivers. Relationships among these three elements are predicated on informational goals; for the receiver, the need for specific information; for the sender, responding to the perceived need for information that the receiver has; and, for the message, the embodiment of the needed information. The sender, therefore, accommodates the receiver in a number of ways by adapting the information in the message so that the receiver can understand it. For example, the sender uses syntactical arrangement to communicate meta-data about the information. That is, the sender can use a more complex sentence structure to enhance the information. For example, a simple sentence communicates a meaning about something; a complex sentence communicates a meaning about the meaning, with the dependent element functioning to provide background or, in some cases, cause for the independent element. Behind the adaptation is the sender's understanding of how the language works to provide meaning. Should the receiver not be familiar with the content, the sender places undue stress on the receiver by using a more complex presentation style that leaves the receiver struggling with both the content and the means of expression. Added to these problems are the problems of the receiver's attitude toward, among other things, the subject, the sender, and the medium, and the cultural contexts of both the sender and the receiver.

Context provides the basis for understanding the communication. At a simple level, context provides the setting for the sentence establishing, for example, antecedents for the pronouns. Context also provides conditions, should there be any, for actions the reader is to take. Consider this example:

If the gauge reads 75, press the red button.

If the receiver is from a culture that needs the context before the action (such as an American receiver), this organization will be effective. If, on the other hand, the receiver comes from a culture that traditionally reads everything before performing an action (such as a German receiver), the dependent element could go at the end:

Press the red button if the gauge reads 75.

This example demonstrates that there can be more to receiver analysis than determining technical competence and educational levels, roles in an organization, and other such information, as well as the receiver's ability to handle complex syntax. That consideration is culture.

Cross-cultural communication involves more than translating or localizing (or both) a text from one language to another. Ideally, translators/localizers translate meaning that includes cultural contexts. But it is not always possible to have such an ideal situation, because of time and budget. Often, when senders write in English for people who read English as a second or third language, they will not use a translator or localizer to provide for the cultural context. We assume that the senders should be able to adapt text to the situation, but such may not always be the case.

This chapter examines one of the cultural issues relating to receiver analysis: selecting language to use that is culturally appropriate for nonnative receivers reading English texts. The questions I want to address are 1) where do these language differences originate and 2) what can senders do about them? After an overview of language, culture, and societies, I discuss language's two kinds of codes (Restricted and Elaborated) and look at discourse elements (metadiscourse) used to establish context. I then present the results of an informal study on organizing a manual for a different culture.

LANGUAGE AND CULTURE

The receiver, if the language the message uses is the receiver's first language, should understand the cultural context from which the message comes. However, if the message's language is not the receiver's first language, the sender should not assume that the receiver is familiar with the cultural context of the message. While more obviously true when the languages are, say English and Chinese, the same problems can exist when the languages are similar (American English and British English) or even the same (American English and American English) when the sender and the receiver are in different cultural groups.

Whether or not the receiver can recognize less obvious sources of meaning (e.g., the cause-effect relationship established by a dependent-independent clause structure), as well as an attitude toward the message built in as part of the culture, creates a difficult communication situation. In writing instructions, the sender may assume that the receiver knows how to do something because, in the sender's social/cultural group, "Everyone knows how to do that." This assumption about knowledge that appears in the language used in the text is really as much a cultural assumption as it is an informational assumption. The result is that the receiver does not understand the message and fails to reach an informational goal.

In every communication situation, the message can represent a new "cultural group" in that it is composed of elements from the sender's cultural group and what the sender perceives as the receiver's cultural group. In the matter of culture, the message represents a culture that is neither totally the sender's nor the receiver's, but a combination or new culture that exists only for the life of the message [1]. This third culture should represent compromises on both parties' parts because of the informational goal: the receiver has an informational goal that the sender recognizes (either a *specific* goal or a *general* goal). That goal drives both sides of the model: the sender creating the message and the receiver processing it. Thus, the situation is one where the third culture is a way for the receiver to reach his or her informational goal as well as a way for the sender to adapt the message based on the receiver's context.

When the sender and the receiver are in different social/cultural groups (both culturally and informationally), the risks of the receiver not reaching the informational goal are increased because the sender may have unintentionally included elements (such as the language used) that could prevent the receiver from reaching the informational goals. The communication is difficult at best when the two participants are members of the same group, but it quickly becomes more difficult when they are members of different groups. Then, the cultures of their own group can influence each participant to the extent that the message is lost or misunderstood. The sender has specific attitudes toward the receiver just as the receiver has specific attitudes about the sender and the message. In discussing attitudes incorporated in the piece's style, we normally refer to the "tone" of the text as that which expresses those attitudes. *Tone,* as commonly understood, relates to word choice, focusing on the connotation of words, rather than on the denotation. And it can be through connotation that senders must be aware of the role culture plays. Consequently, the sender must select connotatively neutral language to use. But word choice is one of several aspects of connotation that the sender must know and use appropriately.

We can also look at whole sentences as containing a sense—that is, what it means—and a relationship with reality—that is, how the words relate to the reality that they are representing. So, sentences have connotation (variable meaning) and denotation (semantic relationship to reality). Seen in this way, *connotation* can convey what the sender meant by the *denotation* or words selected to convey that meaning. With tone being conveyed by connotation, the total sense of the communication becomes even more important. Words and sentences have a relationship with reality established through the denotative meaning. At this level, the correspondences between what was said and the reality being represented are semantically identifiable. Dictionaries, for example, are repositories of denotation meanings for words. The problems occur at the sense level of the words or sentences. This level, the connotative, has no correspondences—semantically or otherwise—with reality. Rather, the correspondences occur at the intentional level—the intent aimed at by the receiver. When the sender limits that intent by not considering the cultural senses the words and sentences convey, miscommunication/misunderstanding occurs.[1]

Further, the sender's selection of data can have cultural implications if the sender is not aware of how a particular culture (the target culture) assembles and regards data to form information. Certainly, the culture of the receiver will determine in large part the schema that the receiver brings to the text, thus adding another reason why the sender must consider the cultural implications of language, among other things. In addition, questions regarding what the receiver considers weight and value of the data must also find a place in the cultural analyses of the receiver. Whether the sender is preparing instructions, a proposal, a report, or any of the many forms of technical communication, he or she must understand the receiver's schema for the communication to be useful.

If we consider the simple instruction used above—*If the gauge reads 75, press the red button*—we can begin to understand something of the role schema play in reading and actions as well as the connotations of the text. Placing the conditional/dependent clause at the beginning fits the anticipated cause-effect patterning the sender perceived in the receiver. Establish cause first and then establish effect (condition followed by action). Thus, the sender is fitting the syntactical structure to the schematic structure of the receiver. In addition, is *reads* so colloquial to American English that the receiver will understand the metaphorical intent of that verb? The receiver "reads" the instruction; but, can the gauge "read" a value? How culturally tied is the meaning of *reads*? Should the author have said *shows* or *indicates*?

Should that schematic structure require a different syntactical structure—*Press the red button if the gauge reads 75*—where the condition (cause) can follow the action (effect), then the sender must recognize such a structural need and pattern sentences accordingly. Should the sender understand that the receiver's culture generates information following the effect-to-cause schema, then the schema

---

[1] Any number of communication theories focus on the sender's intent (speech-act, for example) so that researchers have a rich field to explore when offering suggestions to authors about what their documents actually communicate. Philosophy also offers discussions on truth values as well as meanings in communications. In addition—and in keeping with definitions for quality (Chapter 2) and culture (Chapter 1)—sentence meaning may be easily identified (as the objective element of a culture and the quantifiable characteristics of quality), or identified with great difficulty (culture's subjective elements and quality's qualitative characteristics).

fits with the sense of the sentence as well as the mapping to reality. Any other pattern will lead to miscommunication.

At the individual word level of the sample instructions, the connotations are neutral—assuming that the receiver's culture does not consider second person offensive. If the schemas of the receiver include considering second person as offensive, then the connotation of the sentence (and the words) contributes to the communication's failure, because the receiver's attention is diverted from the reality represented in the instruction to the offensive part and leads to the receiver being, at best, puzzled as to the sense.

LANGUAGE AND SOCIETIES

A message consists of words; the structural arrangement of those words; the context from which the words come; and the attitudes, values, and thought patterns underlying the words. Both the sender and the receiver operate in this linguistic-cultural environment. One problem for the technical communicator, as I mentioned above, is that the message parts for the receiver whose first language is not English originate in a setting different from that of the sender whose first language is English. Even when the receiver does speak English as a first language but resides in a different culture (e.g., British), differences occur that can influence the receiver's understanding of the message. The question is where do these differences originate and what can the communicator do about them? Later (Chapter 5), I will look at one such set of differences.

There are many theories as to how communication works [2]. One theory that was popular in the early part of the last century was the Sapir-Whorf hypothesis. Essentially, they argued that the structure of your language will influence how you think. With behavior at one level dependent on thought, your native language will have considerable influence on how you behave.

If the goal of the communication is to modify the receiver's conscious behavior (as most instructions try to do) rather than to modify the receiver's cognitive structures,[2] then part of the communication

---

[2] Is the informational goal of the sender to change the behavior of the receiver? It seems that this is one of several possible goals. Another could be that the sender wants to supply information only, and using that information is totally up to the individual. In the first instance (change behavior), the sender is much more aggressive than in the second instance (information only). These two different goals can easily influence all stages of the writing of the document from selecting data to analyzing the receiver to page layout and design.

must accommodate that change in the receiver's schema. When the schema, and hence the behavior, are rooted in the native language (as Sapir and Whorf would have it), then the sender must find ways within the schema to effect a change that will lead to modified or new behavior.

The problem lies in the relationship between language and the schema used to understand that language. One approach is through consciousness, and one approach to understanding consciousness [3] holds that consciousness is the product of a *gestalt* of brain cells, that is, large groups of brain cells working together to produce what we call consciousness. One product of that consciousness is the schema used by the person to develop information from data. We often associate what we know as reality with our consciousness, so that if there is that connection and there is a connection between language and consciousness at both the connotative and denotative levels, then there is something to the idea that the language structure you have as the first language can influence how you behave toward and understand reality. Language habits, then, could predispose choices that you make, both consciously and subconsciously, and the grammatical structure therefore shapes the thought processes. As I will indicate later in this chapter, when we define culture as both subjective and objective structures, the grammar and associated rules of a language are part of the culture's objective elements while the sense generated by the word group (its connotation) can easily be subjective, especially when the word group violates some aspect of the cultural expectations. Both the sender and the receiver each live in and are shaped by a culture. They have their attitudes, beliefs, and values influenced by those same objective and subjective cultural elements. One manifestation of those elements is language, so that if the sender and the receiver are from different cultural groups, the way language works for each will also be different.

With this discussion as background, we can look more closely at language, especially the codes used in communicating both the sense and the reality relationship.

RESTRICTED AND ELABORATED CODES

Two kinds of language found in messages that have cultural implications are Restricted and Elaborated Codes [4]. Restricted Codes are language that everyone using it in the group understands without expansion or explanation. Elaborated Codes are language needing additional explanation and expansion so that everyone in the group can understand. For example, to musicians, *pitch* means something different than it means to a construction worker. If the construction worker told the musician that the roof's pitch needed to be increased, the musician would probably be confused and might not understand. Bernstein's Elaborated/Restricted Code theory, therefore, suggests, among other things, that if someone who is from a group that predominately uses one kind of code tries to communicate with someone from a group that predominately uses another kind of code, miscommunication—at best—is the result. The scientific research article is another example. When the information is for peer scientists, the language is highly specialized and Restricted, and the peer scientists understand the linguistic "short-hand" used to convey complex ideas (e.g., the Methods section). When the information is for the nonpeer, the sender must use a more nonspecialized, Elaborated language. The same phenomenon happens in other areas such as business organizations [5]. When senders use appropriate language codes for their receivers, not only is communication more effective, but also the stability of the cultural group is reinforced.[3]

Extrapolate this conclusion from the middle-class and working-class teens Bernstein used in Britain to communicating across cultural boundaries, say, when someone in the United States tries to communicate with someone in Saudi Arabia. Does the sender take on the code system of the receiver in order to communicate and reach the sender's communication goal (which is either to change behavior or supply information or modify cognitive structures)? Or to help the receiver achieve a communication goal?

Bernstein's theory of codes applies to oral communication (for consistency, I will refer to the initiator of the communication as the sender whether the communication is oral or written). He analyzed the oral communication of two groups of English youth and discovered that they used language specifically reflective of their own culture. Elaborated Codes allow the receiver many different ways of saying something, and these explanations can be involved and lengthy. In order to communicate using Elaborated Codes, the sender must plan carefully—either consciously or subconsciously—just what to say and how to say it. For example, among the simplest of all

---

[3] What is interesting is that most "codes" in technical communication are technical, so the "cultural" element is familiarity with the technical concepts behind the technical terms.

expressions in English are sentences with single subjects, verbs, and objects: *The tool opens the box.* When the sentence becomes complex in structure through adding dependent/subordinate elements, the sender must be aware of where the sentence is going: *When the tool opens the box, ...* What comes next? Or consider the gauge reading and subsequent action: *Press the red button* is a simple action; *When the gauge reads 75 . . .* adds more elaboration through sentence complexity requiring more cognitive processing on the part of both the sender and the receiver. In these sentences, the sender imposes a cause-effect relationship through the sentence structure so that the receiver has to understand that one part is the cause or context and the other is the effect. The receiver must either hold the conditions in memory while processing the main word group, or hold the action in memory when processing the conditions.

These sentences also describe a more complicated reality, one where the sender imposes a judgment/evaluation on events by establishing conditions, and the receiver must recognize and respond to it. When the sender assumes that the receiver will not know the context (from the text or brought to the text from outside it by the receiver), the sender must use extra wording to provide the receiver the context. Thus, the sender must explain matters such as which button to push, which gauge, and what unit of measurement as well as whether the reading is a positive or negative "75." When the sender assumes that context does not solve these issues, the result is an elaborated document that requires more material and is longer and more complex than documents using Restricted Codes, where the sender assumes that context will provide this information. Compare the length and language used in a trouble-shooting guide for a hard drive aimed at a technician with the same guide aimed at a lay reader.

By contrast, Restricted Code language offers a narrow range of options that, along with the meanings of the words and phrases, have been agreed to by the members of the group. There will be no confusion or ambiguity about context in Restricted Code documents, therefore, making them shorter and simpler. Group members understand the context of the message, so the sender provides little to no explanation. If the sender is targeting technicians who have received training in monitoring gauges, the shorter, Restricted Code document will be the result.

Can the same situation found in oral communication be found in written communication? In writing, whether on paper or on screen, the receiver has the time to review, to think, and to look for supplemental material (in a glossary, for example). How can the kind of codes that the sender uses create effective or confusing communication situations? I think that the answers lie in the level of consciousness where reading occurs. For example, receivers have at least two elements in a sentence to process: 1) The form the sentence takes, and 2) the content or ideas. Underlying both is culture.

The Form

Form refers to the structures imposed through language on the words used to produce both sense and a view of reality. At one level, form can refer to the complexity of sentences—simple, compound, complex, compound-complex in English. It can also relate to the rhetorical techniques used to present the information—both their presence and absence (if the receiver needs a definition and it is not provided, that is a rhetorical technique failure by the sender). From our understanding of trying to match the level of technical detail with the receiver's ability to understand it, we learn that when the receiver has relatively little experience with the technical content, senders provide aids to understanding (definitions, additional visuals, analogies, shorter sentences and paragraphs, simpler sentence and paragraph structure—to name but a few). Adding these aids helps the receiver to understand and complete his or her information goals.

Because language involves culture, the way the receivers process the message reflects communication patterns found in the language. So, the forms selected by senders echo the forms common to the language. When both sender and receiver are from the same language culture, both understand how the forms work. But when they are from different language cultures, the potential for misunderstanding increases.

The Content

Initially, the sender must be aware of the technical content of the document—does the receiver understand that content? The problem occurs when the sender does not add the cultural aspects to the equation. Here is where Bernstein's ideas of language codes can prove useful to the sender communicating across cultures. Does the sender understand the kind of language codes common to the receiver's culture, and if so, how does he or she adapt the text to that culture?[4]

Both form and content operate to produce meaning for the text. As mentioned above, the text has to make sense through its relationship with reality. When dealing with content, senders can examine it as to how it relates to the target receiver's culture. What is much harder is for the sender to analyze form in the receiver's culture so as to adapt form in the text to those cultural expectations.

When, therefore, the receiver struggles to understand content (needs information—rarely does the receiver turn to the text to verify things), the form must accommodate the cultural schema used by the receiver. The problem is one of essentially creating a third schema through the document. The receiver, who is reading in English as his or her second language, must modify the language schema of the native language, while the sender need not do so at first. When the two come together through the document creating this third culture, there is also a third schema, a third set of connotations, a third set of cultural sensitivities, and so forth. Deciding which code system to use is that first step for the sender.

OPEN ROLE CULTURES/
CLOSED ROLE CULTURES

When you shift your focus from the language of the groups to the culture they represent, you see a relationship between how the culture views its members and the codes they use. In Bernstein's terms, these societies (or cultures, as I will call them) are open cultures and closed cultures.

Open role cultures offer the individual much more choice. Roles are not set in these groups, and many kinds of behavior are tolerated. The codes used are Elaborated because a great deal must be explained, particularly in behavior. In closed role cultures, the alternatives allowed for individuals are quite limited. These cultures are often gender-based: women do women's work, men do men's work, for example. The roles of the individuals are often set by a culture and that restricts behavior. We also find an economic use of language

---

[4] An even more interesting issue is the ability of the receiver whose first language is not English to switch schemas depending on the language in use. That issue, however, is for another book.

because of the Restricted Codes that make it up. Identity comes from the culture itself and individualism is discouraged. Something similar appears in the work of Hofstede [6].

Various socializing forces are at work to ensure that the type of group is maintained. These forces are the family, school, peers, work environment and colleagues, religion, and so on. When someone exceeds the limits imposed by these forces through either trying to take on a new role or using different language codes, the forces will exert pressure through, among other means, language for that individual to conform. It works for both types—open/Elaborated, closed/Restricted. With closed role/Restricted Code groups there is pressure to reject individualistic roles and language that encourages individualism. But even in cultures where Elaborated Codes and open roles are encouraged, pressures from the culture push the individual to use Elaborated Codes and take on different roles. The technical communicator, therefore, must carefully word the documents to accommodate both the culture and the language codes used.

Because of the need for technical communicators to make information available to those who need it in a form that they can use, technical communicators, when writing instructions, can be seen as translating Restricted Codes into Elaborated Codes or possibly one set of Restricted Codes (the action plus all the technical reasons for the action that are not expressed) to another set of Restricted Codes (the actions alone). The nature of the culture—open or closed—also influences the communication. Does the text contribute to maintaining the cultural nature of the receiver or does it violate it? But, as with any generalization, saying cultures are open-role/Elaborated Code groups and closed-role/Restricted Code groups describes more an ideal than a reality. In reality, groups are mixed, but it is possible to detect general trends so that useful target group analysis (especially relating to the culture of the group) becomes even more important.

EXAMPLE: A SURVEY ON WAYS OF ORGANIZING A MANUAL FOR A DIFFERENT CULTURE

Let me now turn to an example. Person A whose second language is English needs information about how to use a piece of graphing software and turns to a document (the manual). Person A is going to interact with that document and, we hope, extract the information needed to complete some task. Our receiver will approach the document and the process of extracting the needed information based on a number of learned patterns. For example, is the individual in an open-role or closed-role society? Does the person normally use Restricted Codes or Elaborated Codes when needing to extract information? Is the culture of which this person is a member a culture where the individual's identity comes from the group or individualistically?[5] And what of the sender? All these questions apply to the sender as well. In addition, the sender decides how to organize the materials in a particular way, what parts of the information to give the receiver and in what forms, and these choices can be culturally driven as well as context- and situation-driven.

Technical communicators are aware of the "standards" for technical communication: keep things simple; get to the point and do not waste the receiver's time, among others. Each of these describes the culture of an American technical communication, a culture that differs from that of A's prevailing culture, but which the prevailing culture has come to accept because A needs this piece of American software. For A, the culture of the English language is not the predominating culture in the society. In fact, it is possible that there are two cultures in the receiver's society just as there are in the writer's: a culture that emerges when information is transferred and a culture that is the general culture, both of which can be objective or subjective. These two cultures may or may not be at odds with each other.

You get much the same thing when you adapt text to specific receivers or classes of receivers. The document reflects a level of knowledge less than the writer has and more than the receiver has. But what happens when the sender is aware that the culture of the receiver is different? The sender, in developing the information, considers the receiver (receiver analysis); and the receiver enters the document out of necessity (need for information). So the two come together through the document. Receivers and writers modify beliefs, attitudes, values, and so on, in order to accomplish their communication goals. The result of these modifications is really that third culture I described above.

---

[5] See Table 2 in Chapter 2 on individual value in a culture.

There is tacit agreement that the information is temporarily more important than the cultural backgrounds and pressures of either receiver or writer. But neither can completely forget or ignore their respective cultures. When the writer must necessarily create this third culture, he or she does not have the benefit of oral conversation to characterize the third culture and allow it to evolve through give and take. So, the writer has to act *both* parts in creating the third culture in the document. The receiver has to overlook a cultural violation (objective or subjective). Thus, the subconscious reading moves to a conscious level and the receiver must decide the amount of disturbance the violation causes versus the need for the information.

For this example, I want to look at how the sender might organize the manual person A has for his software. While the survey described here is far from empirically sound, it does give some interesting insights into how the respondents thought of their own culture, what they believed to be the most important cultural element driving how they would organize the manual, and what they believed the best organizational pattern would be.

Introduction to the Survey

With the understanding of codes and culture as background, let me turn to an informal survey I conducted at FORUM95, November 1995, in Dortmund, Germany, and subsequently at the tekom (the German technical communication society) conference that followed in Dortmund, as well as at a guest lecture at the University of Paderborn. One culturally determined area where the technical communicator can accommodate different cultures is how the document is organized. At a simple level, the document's organization can follow the pattern discussed above for placing causes and effects in sentences. Does the receiver need the big picture first or second or not at all? Does the sender, when organizing the document, move deductively or inductively? Culturally determined schemas will influence how that document will be assembled. So, my goal in the survey was to find out if, in fact, practicing professional technical communicators consider these matters when organizing a document.

Method

I presented information on cross-cultural communication to those attending the FORUM95 conference, the tekom conference immediately following FORUM95, and a lecture at the University of

Paderborn (all in Germany). The presentation consisted of a short talk on cross-cultural issues, focusing on the cultural implications of time,[6] followed by a survey in which the listeners could apply the information from the talk by organizing a manual intended for traditional Eastern audiences.

The survey was in two parts: part I asked demographic information about the participant concerning the person's culture, and part II provided four organizational patterns[7] for a table of contents for the manual. Based on what they "learned" from the brief talk and their own experiences, they were to select an organizational pattern for the manual or suggest one of their own. The manual was for a software product (fictional) that allowed the receiver to develop graphic representations of data.

Results

Learning how a person identifies his or her culture, while not an immediate objective of the survey, showed some possible insights into problems in recognizing the culture of the reader during reader analysis. Table 1 shows the answers categorized into abstract classes. A look at these categories shows that a wide variety of perceptions exist based on the idea of what a culture really is. None of the categories are mutually exclusive; they reflect the more objective elements of classifying/defining/identifying a culture. For example, a typical response to the question would be to name a country (Germany) as the respondent's culture. I then abstracted the answer to "Geographical Region." This question appeared only on the FORUM95 survey because those attending the FORUM95 conference were technical communicators from a variety of countries, whereas those attending the tekom presentation following FORUM95 and those attending the lecture at the University of Paderborn were German.

I was also curious to know what were the main cultural elements they considered when writing a manual. Tables 2 and 3 show those

[6] See Table 1 in Chapter 2 for a summary of views about time.

[7] The provided patterns were as follows: Pattern I: Getting Started, Using the Program, Technical Information, Frequently Asked Questions; Pattern II: Using the Program, Getting Started, Technical Information, Frequently Asked Questions; Pattern III: Technical Information, Frequently Asked Questions, Getting Started, Using the Program; Pattern IV: Frequently Asked Questions, Using the Program, Getting Started, Technical Information.

Table 1. Responses on Cultures of Respondents
(FORUM95 Only)

Categories of response	Number (N = 43)	%
No answer	9	21
Politics	8	19
Religion	8	19
Geographical region	6	14
Profession	6	14
Social group	6	14

Table 2. Main Cultural Element Considered
When Writing a Manual

Response	Number (N = 43)	%
No answer	25	58
Named an element (see Table 3); no individual element received more than one mention	18	48

Table 3. Cultural Elements Mentioned

Culturally explicit examples	Method of reading
Simple language	Politeness
Human-oriented society	Technology background more important than culture
Education—previous knowledge	
Style	Language, graphical information
Standards	Ability to translate
Organization	Make my own text clear
Level of details	All language skills of receivers
	No answer (3)

results. In other words, given the assignment where they had to prepare a manual for a culture other than their own, what cultural element(s) did they consider to be the main factor influencing how they prepared the manual? Again, only those at FORUM95 responded.

I received a total of 86 survey forms from all three locations. Most participants (52%) chose one of the provided organizational patterns, with "Other Organizational Patterns" receiving 42% (see Table 4). I asked those selecting the latter response to specify what the pattern should be. Table 5 shows the most frequently cited patterns.

I asked each group (as a conclusion to the talk) to suggest ways that communicators could make their documents more culturally effective. Tables 6, 7, and 8 show the responses.

Discussion

The results show that none of the provided organizing patterns received overwhelming support. "Other" received the largest percentage of responses, but still under half. The drop from "Other" to the numbered patterns is suggestive. Those participants offering their own organizational pattern believed that the organizing patterns offered in the survey were inadequate to meet the needs of the target group. Such a result suggests that they were thinking about how best to accommodate the informational needs of their target receivers. But were the suggested alternatives the result of considering the culture of the target audience or only what the participant thought would be the most effective organization regardless of culture? Were the respondents considering only how they would organize the manual for receivers in their own cultures? The survey does not answer those questions.

While I have no empirical basis to suggest that the presentations and lecture were not influential (I had no control group), I do think that the material I presented made little impression on the survey responses. If the culture into which the sample manual was to be sent was a traditional Eastern culture, then an organizational pattern that provided considerable background explanation before getting to the actual operation should have some prominence. Pattern IV comes closest to that fit (with the possible alternative of switching FAQ and Getting Started).

Table 4. Organizational Methods Selected by Respondents

Organizational method	FORUM95: Idea Market (N = 14)	FORUM95: Sort-and-Build (N = 10)	FORUM95: Total (N = 24)	tekom (N = 47)	Paderborn (N = 15)	Grand total (N = 86)
I	7%	10%	8%	15%	20%	14%
II	0%	40%	17%	11%	7%	12%
III	7%	40%	21%	17%	7%	16%
IV	36%	10%	25%	11%	9%	13%
Other	36%	0%	21%	47%	60%	42%
No answer[a]	14%	0%	8%	9%	7%	3%

[a] Respondents did not suggest an organizing pattern but did respond to the demographic questions.

Table 5. Patterns Offered as "Other"

14%	8%	5%	5%
Getting Started	Frequency Asked Questions	Frequency Asked Questions	Technical Information
Using the Program	Technical Information	Getting Started	Getting Started
Frequently Asked Questions	Getting Started	Using the Program	Using the Program
Technical Information	Using the Program	Technical Information	Frequently Asked Questions

Table 6. Responses from FORUM95 Participants on Making Documents more Culturally Effective

Idea Market[a]	Sort-and-Build Group[b]
Collaboration	Know cultural taboos
Testing using nontraditional methods	Style—sentence and paragraph structure, attitudes (tone)
Local technical writer	Contextuality
Local editor	Visual rather than verbal orientation

[a]The Idea Market is a concept unique to FORUM conferences. In a large room, 10 to 12 "stands" are set with two flipcharts for each. The presenter stands in front of the charts and gives a brief summary of the topic to attendees who cluster around the stand (there are no chairs). The first chart displays a visual summary. Then the group discusses the points the speaker raises and the speaker keeps notes on the second chart. The original points plus the results of the discussion are later combined into a conference publication called the *PostHarvest*.

[b]If the attendees around a particular speaker believe there is much more to discuss after the time expires, they can request a room for what is called a "Sort-and-Build Group." They then continue their discussion, and the speaker, as leader, records their comments and includes them in the *PostHarvest* publication.

Certainly, this informal survey offers no conclusive results and generalizations about organizing manuals. More controlled experiments should establish definitive answers. This survey, however, did offer some interesting insights into issues of cross-cultural communication.

Table 7. Responses from tekom Participants on Making
Documents More Culturally Effective

Session I	Session II	Session III
Collaboration—sample from group	How many calls to Help Desk	Rewritten by native
Usability testing; native editor	Usability testing—in target country	Research cultural background
Survey of some kind	Have locating information/key words in index	Consult translators who know culture
Native writers		Documentation should reflect the culture of
Module construction	Sales figures	the product[a]

[a]When asked to explain this rather unusual suggestion, the participant said that all products carry a culture of one kind or another. In this case—the BusinessGraph example—software designed to save the receiver time would, perhaps, have problems in cultures where saving time is not important, if the manual emphasized the time-saving features of the product—an excellent point.

Table 8. Conclusion Offered at
Paderborn University on Making
Documents More Culturally Effective

Collaboration in several forms

Usability testing

Native editor

Awareness of target culture

[a]In Paderborn, I summarized what I thought were the consensus responses.

REFERENCES

1. F. L. Casmir, Third-Culture Building: A Paradigm Shift for International and Intercultural Communication, *Communication Yearbook*, no. 16, Sage, Newbury Park, California, pp. 407-457, 1993.
2. S. W. Littlejohn, *Theories of Human Communication* (7th Edition), Wadsworth, Belmont, California, 2002.

3. S. A. Greenfield, *Journey to the Centers of the Mind: Toward a Science of Consciousness,* W. H. Freeman and Company, New York, 1995.
4. B. Bernstein, *Class, Codes, and Control,* vol. I: *Theoretical Studies Toward a Sociology of Language,* Routledge and Kegan Paul, London, 1971.
5. C. Morrill, Decoding the Language of Etzioni's Moral Dimensions in Complex Organizations, in *Macro Socio-Economics: From Theory to Activism,* D. Sciulli (ed.), M. E. Sharpe, Armonk, New York, pp. 195-216, 1996.
6. G. Hofstede, *Cultures and Organizations: Software of the Mind,* McGraw-Hill Book Company, New York, 1991; Cultural Predictors of National Negotiation Styles, in *Processes of International Negotiation,* F. Mautner-Markhof (ed.), Westview Press, Boulder, Colorado, pp. 193-201, 1989; *Culture's Consequences: International Differences in Work-Related Values,* Sage, Beverly Hills, California, 1987.

CHAPTER 4

Communicating Style Rules
to Editors of
International Standards

Poorly written instructions are constantly confronting us, and the problems of clarity become even more apparent when these instructions cross international boundaries. For example, poor instructions for programming a VCR or assembling a bicycle create frustration regardless of whether readers in the United States or readers in other countries use them. We know from anecdotal evidence of instances where something has gone bad because the documents do not make sense or offend a cultural attitude: automobile companies change car names, advertising agencies revise campaigns, and so on. Among the areas where the potential problem can lead to much more than a chuckle is in communicating international standards.

Few authors pay attention to language when they draft documents meant to be standards. While draft standards pass through many reviews before being accepted as a standard, the reviews often focus only on the technical matters, although some comments occasionally relate to language and usage. For the International Organization for Standardization Technical Committee 184, Sub-Committee 4 (ISO TC 184/SC4), a Quality Committee (QC) controls the quality of the draft documents. It formerly reviewed the drafts for compliance to established writing standards, and under this older quality control system, QC members spent an extraordinary amount of time reviewing and editing the draft documents—many running to over

3,000 pages. Because this reviewing/editing slowed approval of the standard, QC redesigned the quality assurance system so that the drafting committees could apply the quality measures themselves as they wrote their draft with a minimum of interference from QC. This new approach involved a series of checklists for the various elements in drafting a standard—a project leaders' checklist, a checklist for internal review, and convenor's (i.e., group chair) checklist.[1]

Authors and editors follow a set of directions from ISO that function as a style guide [2]. These directives are supplemented by a QC document that expands and clarifies the ISO requirements [3]. These two documents form the basic style guides for preparing TC 184/SC4 draft international standards. Thus, the project authors and editors have guidelines to use to ensure the quality in their documents, and each working group and each project team within a working group must read, understand, and apply the guidelines when producing a draft so as to be able to complete the checklists. They certify their compliance to both the *ISO Directives—Part 3* and the QC *Supplementary Directives* by submitting completed and signed checklists.

The *Supplementary Directives (SDs)* and checklists, as well as the standards themselves, must be written in British English (following *The Concise Oxford Dictionary* [4]). The *SDs* themselves, as well as the checklists, must be written for the project team members (leaders, authors, and editors) not expert in editing. The documents' readers have no real need to be persuaded that they should follow the procedures outlined in the SDs and the *ISO Directives—Part 3,* 1997, because their draft will not be approved until they certify through the checklists that the draft conforms to the requirements. Thus, like any other style guide meant for the nonexpert, the *SDs* and the parent document, *ISO Directives—Part 3,* 1997, must provide style rules and examples for preparing documents that users will read, understand, and follow. The question is, how easily can the volunteer author(s) or editor(s) read, understand, and apply these key documents when preparing their draft international standards?

This study, therefore, examines selected documents published by ISO QC as well as an example of a draft standard from another

---

[1] For information on how a draft document becomes an international standard as well as the various documents that authors and editors of draft standards can use, see the ISO TC 184/SC4 website. Click on "Necessary Documents" and "Standardization Process Summary" [1].

international body associated with ISO to see whether they are written so as to be usable by the authors and editors who prepare draft international standards.

LANGUAGE CODES AND
METADISCOURSE

Because the style manuals must be read and understood by project leaders, authors, and editors whose first language may not be English, the way that they are written becomes extremely important. Those who prepare these style guides can improve understanding by realizing that their readers come from a linguistically diverse environment. One aspect of the linguistics landscape that can be a useful analytical tool is the language codes commonly used. Bernstein's system of Restricted and Elaborated Codes [5] offers one approach to understanding that landscape (see also the discussion of these codes in Chapter 3). Applying these codes to the way communication is structured can help authors and editors enhance their communication quality. A second useful analytical tool is metadiscourse. In the following sections I first discuss Berstein's codes and then metadiscourse.

Language Codes

In 1971, Basil Bernstein interviewed a group of youths in England and tape-recorded their conversations. From these tapes, he discovered that the youths fit into two distinct cultural groups and that these groups approached communication differently. One group was relatively closed to outsiders and used language codes that they all seemed to understand without a lot of explanation, so the quantity of the individual communication among them was limited. This method of communication also serves to exclude outsiders, thus reinforcing the view that the group members are special. The second group used a communication style that was much more verbal, containing more quantity than found in the first group. Bernstein called the language used by the first group Restricted Codes and the language of the second Elaborated Codes (Table 1 summarizes the characteristics).

Restricted/Elaborated Code theory suggests, among other things, that communication breaks down when someone who is from a group that predominately uses one kind of code tries to communicate with someone from a group that predominately uses another kind of code.

Table 1. Summary of Expected Characteristics of
Restricted and Elaborated Codes

Feature	Restricted Codes	Elaborated Codes
Phrases	Long	Short
Word length	Short	Long
Verb phrases	Some	Lots
Passive voice verbs	Few	Lots
Uncommon adverbs and adjectives	Few	Lots
Potential audience	Restricted to group members	Expanded beyond the immediate group

A good example is the progress report directed within a company to an immediate supervisor. In this report, the author needs only to remind the reader of the context, goals, and tasks, without a need for extensive definitions of technical terms, simplified visuals, detailed explanations of goals and tasks, and so on. Statements relating to tasks completed, ongoing, and yet to be done need not necessarily contain explanations of procedures and activities because the reader should know what they are, unless there is something highly specialized or modified for this particular occasion. The document's target audience is a person whose background and experiences as well as corporate culture are similar to the author's. Should, for whatever reason, the progress report need to be sent to other readers whose backgrounds, experiences, and corporate culture are not similar to the author's (an engineer writing for an external client, for example), the report would be a lot different and lot longer, with the author adding explanations and other materials. The same phenomenon happens in other written and oral communication situations (for a discussion of codes in business organizations, see Morrill [6]).

The structural equivalent of Restricted/Elaborated Codes is the syntax of a sentence. When authors assume that the readers fully understand all aspects of the sentence, they can use more simplified sentences. When the readers need more information, the authors must elaborate through adding phrases/clauses. Consider the following example: *The report is due next Friday.* When readers know what *report* and which *Friday,* as well as the consequences, authors can state the information in the simplest possible terms. If the assumed reader does not know the context (in whole or in part), the author must elaborate on the concepts. The form that the elaborated information will take depends on the kind of elaboration needed and its relationship to the main assertion. The sentence could become complex in structure through adding dependent/subordinate elements, giving the author the opportunity to elaborate on the simple expression: *While the report is due next Friday, . . .* An instruction such as *Type your name in the space provided* tells the reader to perform an action. Authors add a level of complexity when writing instructions, because one or more parts of the sentence are inferred (use of *you* as the subject, for example). As before, if the reader does not know the context, the author can elaborate. *When you type your name in the space provided . . .* adds even more complexity requiring more cognitive processing on the part of the reader/user. In the complex sentence construction, the author assumes that the reader/user does not know enough about the situation or needs some preconditions unknown to the reader and so imposes a cause-effect relationship through the sentence structure. The user has to understand that one part is the cause or context and the other is the effect. Often, metadiscourse introduces such complexity. When the author assumes that the user will not know the context, you will find extra wording to tell the user of that context.

In Chapter 3, we looked at applying Bernstein's codes to a written context (his was an oral one) and found that authors can gain insight into producing better documents through a careful analysis both of the knowledge base of the reader and of the cultural context and subsequent schema. In addition, we saw that miscommunication can happen when the author uses the wrong codes—both vocabulary and sentence structure—so that the reader's reading becomes conscious while trying to cope with both content issues and form issues. Thus, we get a situation where the complex sentence can be restrictive (because the author sets conditions) when compared with the compound sentence or paired simple sentences, and elaborated when compared with the single simple sentence.

The second element (the first is the language codes) is the language selected. From our understanding of trying to match the level of technical detail with the user's ability to understand it, we learn that when the user has relatively little experience with the technical content, authors provide aids to understanding (advanced organizers, definitions, additional visuals, analogies, longer sentences and paragraphs, and more complex sentence and paragraph structure, to name but a few elaboration devices). Adding these aids helps the user understand and more easily satisfy his or her information goals. A key element (or tool) the author can use is metadiscourse.

Metadiscourse and Its Role

There is some confusion over the exact definition of metadiscourse (see, e.g., Mao [7]). Generally, though, most researchers seem to agree that it functions to help readers understand text and that it advances the proposition of the text in some way. Metadiscourse is an Elaborated Code device used by authors to keep their readers reading, and its aids the reader in processing the text by providing hints on how to consider the text.

Authors use metadiscourse to make clear certain supplemental meanings they wish to communicate (we could even say that, to some extent, metadiscourse supports the connotation sense of the sentence). These meanings could be attitudes toward text and reader, the author's organizational approach, and so on. Text without metadiscourse would be text that the author assumes the reader fully understands on its own—that is, completely Restricted Code text. One example of a document with no metadiscourse is a note you write to yourself: Get milk. You should not need to add metadiscourse, as the text itself would be sufficient for you to understand.

Several researchers [e.g., 7-9] have classified the various forms of metadiscourse beyond the simple category of *transitions*. The most elaborate system is that of Vande Kopple [8], who, in a presentation to the Conference on College Composition and Communication, identified 6 major groups of metadiscourse devices with 17 subgroups and 13 sub-subgroups. Longo [9] presents a simpler approach similar to Vande Kopple's. She had 3 major groups (Text Connectives, Code Glosses, and Illocution Markers) and 10 subcategories (6 under Text Connectives, 3 under Code Glosses, and 1 under Illocution Markers). Table 2 shows that the two systems offer a wide range of metadiscourse items that function to elaborate the texts.

ISO/QC Documents

If the style guide documents contained material about the technical subjects of the standards, the authors could use Restricted Codes. But the style documents discuss style matters, and the users are

Table 2. Classification Systems of Vande Kopple and Longo

Vande Kopple [7]	Longo [9]
Text Connectives	**Text Connectives**
Sequence	Logical connectors
Logical or temporal relationship	Temporal connectors
Reminder of materials presented earlier	Reminders
Forthcoming material	Announcements
Topicalizers	Topicalizers
	Sequencers
Code Glosses	**Code Glosses**
Definition	Definitions
Problem with ordinary interpretation of words	Explanation
How readers should take words	Delimiting
Help readers interpret troublesome passages	
Explanatory detail about figures and charts	
Illocution Markers	**Illocution Markers**
Make specific action explicit	Examples
Modify amount of force	
Soften force	
Tag questions	
Increase force	
Epistemological Markers	
Modality markers	
Shields	
Emphatics	
Punctuation marks	
Evidentials	
Personal beliefs	
Induction	
Deduction	
Sensory experience	
From other's work	
Attitude Markers Commentary	
Comment on reader's mood	
Recommend mode of reading	
Address questions	
Comment on hoped-for-stance by reader	

outside their areas of expertise and may range from highly knowledgeable about language and editing to novices. In the context of Bernstein's Restricted and Elaborated Codes, the samples fall into a communication situation where the authors of the style guides and their readers are not members of the same expertise group—that is, the expected groups are members of a scientific/technical group that understands technical language (e.g., those in an automotive standards group understand automotive terminology and concepts) but not necessarily editing concepts. The communication problem for the authors of the sample style guides is that they must address not this closed group of technical experts who understand what is being communicated (i.e., the correct style for a draft standard), but a cross-section of experts from all disciplines represented in this standards community.

METHOD OF ANALYSIS

In deciding on which metadiscourse classification system to use, I looked at the context for the samples. As I indicated above, the readers of these documents did not need to be persuaded to accept the validity of the information, nor did the authors need to be concerned about the attitudes of the readers toward either the subject or themselves. Likewise, the statements made in the samples were assertions not needing support (i.e., reasons for the assertion, proof for the validity of the assertion, etc.). That left only the need for the readers to understand and apply the text easily. Given these circumstances, I selected to use the simpler approach to classifying the metadiscourse markers (see Table 2, Longo's system of classification).

Samples

I selected as samples passages from documents produced for the international standards community by committees of the ISO and the International Electrotechnical Commission (IEC).[2] They are samples from the ISO/QC "style guides" and from a draft standard produced by IEC on writing technical manuals for electromechanical devices. All samples are introductory in nature—that is, they come from front matter meant to set the tone and context for what follows. I examined

[2] I have included the sample from the draft standard from IEC because of access restrictions. For the other sample texts, see reference 3.

the codes used and the number of words, sentences, and paragraphs; sentence structure; and amount and kinds of metadiscourse.

As mentioned before, the readers of these ISO/QC guides are persons who are experts in the technical subject matter of the draft standard. The IEC sample actually addresses technical communicators who produce manuals for electrotechnical equipment (e.g., transformers and the like); that sample is not from a style guide but from an actual draft international standard. Presumably, the authors are "experts" in communicating (language and editing). Therefore, one would expect the readers of the IEC example (S-1; see Appendix 4-1, p. 66) to find Restricted Codes, while readers of the ISO/QC documents (S-2, S-3, and S-4) would expect Elaborated Codes. In terms of metadiscourse, the IEC document should have fewer and more restricted examples than the ISO/QC documents.

In both sets of examples, one would not expect to find the kinds of metadiscourse associated with situations where the reader must be persuaded to accept the text and its arguments (as in a proposal). All the examples come from contexts where the reader would have already accepted the need to use the material or would not be reading it at all. So, the metadiscourse of the examples should center on text connectives and code glosses, with little in the way of illocutionary, validity, attitude, and similar markers. For classifying sentence structure into simple, compound, complex, and compound-complex, I use traditional labeling of word groups based on subject, verb, and object, etc.

RESULTS

Tables 3 to 9 show the results of the analysis. As Table 3 shows, all samples had long sentences (ranging from 18.6 words per sentence for S-2 to 52.2 words per sentence for S-3). Simple sentences dominated S-1, S-2, and S-3, with complex and compound-complex sentences appearing in S-4. (Interestingly, the complex sentence structure was also a feature of S-1, with 39% of the sentences being complex.) Paragraphs were likewise rather long (from 49.9 words per paragraph for S-1 to 94 words per paragraph for S-3). The amount of metadiscourse varied a great deal from 0.4% of the total words (S-3) to 21.5% of the total words (S-4). In all four samples, the type of metadiscourse used was quite limited: connectives. Samples S-2, S-3, and S-4 had only connectives, while S-1 had glosses and illocutionary markers as well as connectives.

Table 3. Comparison of the Four Samples

Item	Expected Codes		Samples			
	Rest.	Elab.	S-1	S-2	S-3	S-4
Sentences						
Number	Fewer	More	18	26	9	3
Clause structure						
Simple	More	Fewer	9 (50%)	22 (84.6%)	5 (55%)	0 (0%)
Compound	Fewer	More	2 (11%)	1 (4%)	2 (22.2%)	0 (0%)
Complex	Fewer	More	7 (39%)	3 (11.5%)	2 (22%)	2 (67%)
Compound-complex	Fewer	More	0 (0%)	0 (0%)	0 (0%)	1 (33%)
Sentences per paragraph	Fewer	More	2.25	4.33	1.8	3
Paragraph						
Number	Fewer	More	8	6	5	1
Words						
Number	Fewer	More	399	483	470	93
Words/sentence	Fewer	More	22.2	18.58	52.22	31.7
Words/paragraph	Fewer	More	49.9	80.5	94	93
					2	4
Metadiscourse					2 (0.4%)	20 (21.5%)
Units	Lower	More	17	9		
Words (% total metadiscourse words)			63 (16%)	39 (8.1%)		
Metadiscourse type						
Connectives			12 (75%)	9 (100%)	2 (100%)	
Glosses			2 (12.5%)	0 (0%)	0 (0%)	
Illocution			2 (12.5%)	0 (0%)	0 (0%)	

Notes: Rest, Restricted Codes; Elab., Elaborated Codes; S-1, IEC "Introduction," see Appendix 4-1; S-2, ISO TC 184/SC4 N537:1997 (E); S-3, ISO/IEC 1997 "Foreword": S-4, ISO/IEC 1997 "Introduction."

Table 4. Interpretation of the Results

Item	S-1	S-2	S-3	S-4
Sentences and paragraphs (number, words per sentence, words per paragraph)	Elaborated	Elaborated	Elaborated	Elaborated
Clause structure	Restricted[a]	Restricted	Restricted	Elaborated
Metadiscourse	Elaborated	Elaborated/ Restricted	Restricted	Elaborated
Totals	2 Elaborated 1 Restricted	1 Elaborated 1 Restricted 1 Combination	1 Elaborated 2 Restricted	Elaborated
Interpretation	More Elaborated than Restricted	Borderline	More Restrictive than Elaborated	Elaborated

[a]S-1 has 39% complex sentences, suggesting Elaborated.

Table 4 shows an overall evaluation of the samples relative to Bernstein's Restricted and Elaborated Codes. The table considers words, sentences and sentence structure, paragraphs, and metadiscourse. Only sample S-4 was consistent in the areas of analysis, while the other samples were mixed.

Table 5 presents the results from applying the analysis to the full version of S-3: the *ISO Directives—Part 3,* 1997, the central style document for authors of draft standards regardless of technical committee or subcommittee. Overall, the sentences were relatively long but the paragraphs were short (words per sentence, 26.1; words per paragraph, 38.8; and sentences per paragraph, 1.5).

Given the context for all four samples, the expectations should have been that sample S-1 (meant for technical communicators) would be more restrictive in style than the other samples. Samples S-2, S-3, and S-4 are used by authors and editors of draft international standards who are not expert in effective communication. Consequently, those samples should reflect a more elaborated style, one that made heavy use of metadiscourse.

Table 5. Analysis of Samples S-3

Item	ISO Directives—Part 3, 1997
Sentences	
Number	364
Clause structure	
Simple	213 (55.2%)
Compound	31 (8%)
Complex	125 (32.4%)
Compound-complex	17 (4.4%)
Sentences per paragraph	1.5
Paragraph	
Number	245
Words	
Number	9,495
Words/sentence	26.1
Words/paragraph	38.8
Metadiscourse	
Number of units	237
Types	
Connectives	114 (48%)
Glosses	16 (7%)
Illocution	107 (45%)

DISCUSSION

The results are skewed in one respect because one sample (S-4, "Introduction") is one paragraph. However, that only affected the average number of words per paragraph. The other results for S-4 were valid. To provide an analysis of a complete document, I evaluated the *ISO Directives—Part 3,* 1997. These results, shown in Table 5, also have some skewing because they are instructions and include samples of boilerplate text that ISO requires. Still, there is enough evidence to suggest that the authors did not pay close attention to the way they presented the information to readers who were not editing experts. The ISO approach for these style guides is that they want as elaborated a style as possible, yet the results of the analysis tell a different story. The style and use of metadiscourse

Table 6. Metadiscourse Elements in IEC Draft International
Standard (S-1)

Sentence	Metadiscourse	Type
1	The purpose of . . .	Text: announcement
2	The means of . . .	Code Gloss: explanation
3	As a means of communication . . .	Text: topicalizer
4	Depending on product characteristics, complexity, risk, and legal requirements . . . . . . for example . . .	Code Gloss: delimiting Illocution: example
5	None	
6	. . . therefore . . . . . . in conjunction with . . . . . . where no such standard exists . . .	Text: connective Text: connective Text: topicalizer
7	Users of this International Standard are reminded . . .	Text: reminder
8	. . . therefore . . .	Text: connective
9	It should be especially noted that . . .	Text: sequence
10	. . . obviously . . . . . . the amount of . . .	Modality Marker (Vande Kopple) Illocution: example
11	. . . therefore . . .	Text: connective
12 to 13	None	
14	For such negotiations . . .	Text: topicalizer
15	It should also be mentioned that the amount of . . .	Text: announcement
16	None	
17	Therefore . . .	Text: connective
18	None	

Table 7. Metadiscourse Elements in
ISO TC 184/SC4 N537:1997(E) (S-2)

Sentence	Metadiscourse	Type
1	None	
2	The objective . . .	Text: announcement
3	The nature of this description . . .	Text: announcement
4	This International Standard is organized . . .	Text: sequencer
5	None	
6	None	
7	The purpose of this Standing Document . . .	Text: announcement
8	This Standing Document specifies . . .	Text: announcement
9	This Standing Document augments . . .	Text: announcement
10	This Standing Document is divided . . .	Text: announcement
11 to 22	None	
23	For these reasons . . .	Text: reminder
24	As with the ISO Directives . . .	Text: reminder
25 to 26	None	

suggest that the style guide authors assumed that their readers are highly competent editors and authors.

The low occurrence of metadiscourse markers allows us to infer that the authors thought the readers would have no problems reading the text. For example, the almost complete absence of code glosses suggests that the authors thought the readers would understand all the terminology used in the directives—regardless of whether it related to editing, the technical details of style, and the technical elements of publishing (this observation is especially true of the metadiscourse markers in the full version of sample S-3).

Table 8. Metadiscourse Elements in ISO/IEC 1997 "Foreword" (S-3)

Sentence	Metadiscourse	Type
1 to 4	None	
5	Furthermore . . .	Text: connective
6	None	
7	. . . but . . .	Text: connective
8 to 9	None	

Table 9. Metadiscourse Elements in ISO/IEC 1997 "Introduction" (S-4)

Sentence	Metadiscourse	Type
1	It is recognized that . . .	Text: topicalizer
2	Therefore, wherever possible . . .	Text: topicalizer
3	. . . it is permitted that . . .	Text: topicalizer
	However, for such cases it should be noted that . . .	Text: topicalizer

CONCLUSIONS

Context plays a significant role in communicating information. When the users of that information come from a context where they are not expert in editing, authors of documents meant for these users can provide help in addition to simplifying the vocabulary. Recognizing that the users may rely on language codes that assume levels of understanding about the text should lead authors to reduce the amount of and change the kind of metadiscourse used. Users from contexts not familiar with such assumptions need more help understanding the text.

In addition, editors of international standards frequently do not have English as their first language, so they need significant help in order to get the standards "right"—at least in such a style and format that they will conform to the ISO requirements. In order to do this, they need to understand such documents as the *10303 Supplementary Directives* and *ISO Directives—Part 3,* 1997. When authors of these style guides take into account the kinds of structural help their readers will need (i.e., text connectives) as well as the contextual backgrounds of the readers, they can construct documents that can be understood by a wide variety of users.

This particular study, ultimately, shows that current documents produced by the standards community are not clearly aimed at one contextual orientation or another. When the Quality Committee revises these, they should consider both the metadiscourse elements and the language codes selected.

APPENDIX 4-1
Sample 1 (S-1)

DRAFT: 61082-11 Ed. 1, IEC 61082
Preparation of documents used in electrotechnology:
Preparation of Instructions (3B/???/CDV © IEC:1998)

Introduction

The purpose of this International Standard is the collection of requirements and methodological rules to be followed when creating instructions for users of products.

Instructions are the means of conveying information to the user on how to use the product in a correct and safe manner. As a means of communication, texts, words, signs, symbols, diagrams, illustrations and audible or visible information are used, separately or in combination.

Depending on product characteristics, complexity, risk and legal requirements, the information for users may be on the product itself or its packaging or in accompanying materials; for example, leaflets, manuals, audio and video tapes, and computer-based presentation, separately or in combination.

No general standard can provide comprehensive information covering each special case. This International Standard, therefore shall be used in conjunction with the requirements of specific product standards, or where no such standards exist, with the relevant requirements of standards for similar products. Users of this International Standard are reminded that some products and the accompanying instruction for their use are subject to statutory regulations that may include special requirements for safety and disposal. This International Standard serves therefore as a frame of reference for future product-specific standards.

It should especially be noted that this standard shall not establish a fixed amount of documentation that has to be delivered together with a product. This would obviously not be possible because this standard shall be valid for all kinds of products but the amount of documentation very much depends on the complexity of the product itself. Therefore this standard lists all possible kinds of instructions one can think of. What this standard does want to standardize is how such instructions shall be prepared if they are existent.

Which instructions will be delivered for a product in many cases results from negotiations between manufacturer/supplier and customer. For such negotiations this standard can serve as a framework listing up all possible kinds of instructions.

It should also be mentioned that the amount of instructions that have to be delivered in many countries depends on regional or national legal regulations, e.g., the EU machine directive.

Assessment of the quality of instructions should follow common criteria. This International Standard therefore has an informative annex containing some practical recommendations and a proposed methodology for assessment. The annexes A, B, and C are addressed primarily to experts engaged in such assessment work; it may also be helpful to the Standard's principal target groups named above.

REFERENCES

1. Http://www.TC184-SC4.org. Select "About TC184/SC4." Then select "About SC4 Standards."
2. *ISO Directives—Part 3,* 1997. http://www.TC184-SC4.org. (For this book, I have left all references to this document as originally published. There is now a new version of the *Directives* that is in only two parts, with Part 2 containing all the material found in the old Part 3.)
3. 10303 Supplementary Directives, 2nd Edition. (QCM243) http://www.TC184-SC4.org.
4. D. Thompson (ed.), *The Concise Oxford Dictionary of Current English* (9th Edition), Clarendon Press, Oxford, 1995.

5. B. Bernstein, *Class, Codes, and Control,* vol. 1: *Theoretical Studies Toward a Sociology of Language,* Routledge and Kegan Paul, London, 1971.
6. C. Morrill, Decoding the Language of Etzioni's Moral Dimensions in Complex Organizations, in *Macro Socio-Economics: From Theory to Activism,* D. Sciulli (ed.), M. E. Sharpe, Armonk, New York, pp. 195-216, 1996.
7. L. R. Mao, I Conclude Not: Toward a Pragmatic Account of Metadiscourse, *Rhetoric Review, 11,* pp. 265-289, 1993.
8. W. J. Vande Kopple, *Refining and Applying Views of Metadiscourse,* paper presented at the 1997 CCCC Convention, Phoenix, Arizona, 1997.
9. B. Longo, The Role of Metadiscourse in Persuasion, *Technical Communication, 41,* pp. 348-352, 1994.

CHAPTER 5

Cultural Influences on Technical Manuals

Whether they are on paper or online, user manuals are the heart of any product because they provide the information the user needs to use the product. Without an understandable manual, the user may cause serious injury or damage; with an understandable manual, the product can do what it was designed to do. Yet, how many manuals end up on dusty bookshelves and are never read?

There are multiple reasons for unused and unread manuals. Certainly, one cause is that something distracts the users while they are reading. One candidate for this distraction is that the communicator did not incorporate cultural considerations when preparing the manual. Therefore, this chapter considers the influences of culture on developing technical documents, specifically manuals.

After identifying some cultural problems, I want to discuss cultural influences using an example of two hypothetical cultures.

SOME CULTURAL PROBLEMS

Communicators can encounter several problems related to culture as they develop their documents. Two of the many are language and user expectations. For example, in instructions written in Western, English-speaking cultural contexts, the principle verb form is the imperative mood where the subject is understood to be the second person *you*—that is, the command form of the verb: *Do this, do that.* In other, non-English-speaking Western cultures, it is considered rude to use second person imperative mood verbs. These are familiar forms used among friends and family and not to be used by strangers—especially authors of texts containing instructions needed for using a product or service. Style can also create problems for the communicator, specifically such matters as word choice, meta-discourse, and sentence structure (see Chapter 4 for a discussion of these issues).

Another cultural problem centers on user expectations. Rhetorically, manuals divide an activity into logical, discrete tasks that the user performs. Again, there can be a cultural element in that arrangement: what constitutes the logical sequence? For example, one culture's users want the overview before moving to the individual tasks, while another culture's users want to get to the tasks immediately. Can we say that one expected approach is more logical than the other? Logic is a subjective element, a cultural relative (see, e.g., [1]). Consequently, the author must have a good understanding of the users' culture when designing the manual so that the information is readily accessible, understandable, and does not offend—all in the cultural terms of the users.

Translations alone cannot address all the issues involved; document developers should modify their work when the users are from a different cultures. Ideally, all manuals are localized during the target culture review by communicators who edit the manual to make sure that the user will not be distracted by cultural issues when wanting to retrieve the needed information to perform a task. But, as we all know, time and budget constraints often make such steps impossible; the authors themselves must be aware of how culture will be involved in the user's search for information.

As we saw with defining *culture* in Chapter 1, a significant part of the definition concerns subjective elements such as values, norms, beliefs, and attitudes [2-4]:

- *Values* are those things that members of a culture deem worthwhile and desirable.
- *Norms,* on the other hand, are the subjective standards that members of a culture identify as being acceptable to those members, especially in patterns of customary behavior.
- A person's *beliefs* are usually associated with the religion the person espouses, or his or her opinions, or both. Individuals believe in the truth of something, and these beliefs can be an instinctive feeling as well as a logical view.

• *Attitudes* are frequently the accepted opinion or way of thinking about something and frequently form the basis for behavior. When we speak about a person's or a culture's views on a topic, we frequently use *attitude* to identify the views.

In addition to these elements, the communicator will find other cultural problems when preparing a document, such as the following:

• Language and style: second person pronouns and sentence structure (when, for English-speaking users, the sentence begins with the condition or result to be followed by the action) are but two difficulties.
• Examples: graphics (even photographs) of taboo objects (a graph example in a graphing software package that shows beef production, and the target users are from a culture that does not eat beef).
• Explanations: benefits (for the individual or the group) and overviews (present or absent).

In what follows, I present an example of how authors can develop profiles of assumed users based on the users' attitudes. I selected *attitude* because it is used most commonly when trying to understand another culture: what is the culture's attitude toward XYZ? In addition, attitudes are often more closely related to the secular aspects of a culture than are the other concepts, and, hence, more likely to be involved when a user reads a manual. Likewise, the communicator can control this particularly subjective aspect more easily than the other concepts.

Any communication must involve a step where the communicator considers user analysis [5]. Normally, user analysis focuses on the tasks the user must perform and assumptions about what the user does and does not know, can and cannot do. If there is time, the communicator analyzes the user based on the ability to process text—in documents or on screen. Rarely does the communicator consider the cultural aspects of the information.

Analyzing the target users for subjective attitudes can be difficult and time-consuming because so many areas are involved in a culture. The following discussion looks at four of these areas because they can have a direct bearing on how communicators develop their documents: knowledge, education, the product, and needs and goals.

Attitude Toward Knowledge

Knowing the attitude of the culture toward knowledge is beneficial because it can help the communicator determine what to develop in the document. How does the culture treat the sources of that knowledge? What sources does the culture find more believable and credible? How can the communicator ensure that the document elicits a positive attitude toward the knowledge it contains?

Attitude Toward Education

Education is important because it helps the communicator understand how to present the materials. Also, the rhetorical situation in a manual is that of teacher and student. So, cultural issues such as the following are important. Who in the culture is educated, when, and how? What is the standard learning process? What are the attitudes toward teachers?

In addition, the style that we select is predicated on the ability of the assumed users to process both the new information and the method used to present it. If the assumed users are struggling with sentence structure (if there is a high percentage of complex sentences, for example), those users could have trouble processing the new information if that new information is more technical than they expected. Added to this style problem are issues related to users whose first language differs from the language of the document.

Attitude Toward the Product

What attitudes do the members of a culture have toward the product? Are they positive? Negative? What is the culture "contained" within the product (see the footnote to Table 7 in Chapter 3)? How much must communicators explain about the importance of the product? What drives the user to the product? Does the user have a high, medium, or low interest in the product? This leads to trying to understand the user's needs for information and purposes for turning to the documentation, both of which can be culturally influenced.

Attitude Toward Needs and Goals

What does the culture say about the person's need for using the product? What are the user's goals? The communicator must show how both the document and the product benefit if not the individual, then the group.

APPLYING CULTURAL ANALYSIS

If we select the cultural elements described above and develop a comparison between two hypothetical cultures, we can get an idea of why it is important to consider culture when designing a manual. Notice how these four elements are substantially *subjective* elements rather than *objective*. That means that the communicator cannot turn to standard references to learn how to prepare a document that will not have cultural distractions.

The two hypothetical cultures represent extremes (see also the Appendix, p. 109) and are not specific to any cultures. For simplicity's sake, I will call them *Culture A* and *Culture B* and will identify the four attitudes discussed above within each one.

Attitude Toward Knowledge

Culture A

Members of Culture A consider knowledge important and useful to fulfill personal goals and objectives, and through fulfilling individual goals and objectives, the group's goals and objectives are also met. These individuals use the knowledge that they gain (essentially through education and training, work experience, or both) for personal needs and ambitions. The culture rewards those who have this knowledge.

Knowledge is essentially generated in the culture from sources external to the individual, with individuals adapting the knowledge to their needs. Relevance of the material is the key for the communicator. Education provides the raw materials, as does experience. Individuals process these raw materials and develop knowledge that they can apply to specific situations. Once they have used that knowledge, it will be put away until another time when it is needed.

Because time spent learning a new product can reduce productivity and hence personal advancement, the user in this culture is eager to get to work, leading to impatience with reading manuals. The well-designed product, according to the views of this culture, should allow immediate and intuitive usage.

For users in this culture, the communicator should indicate how the user can apply the knowledge (to other and similar situations, for example). The examples should be directly relevant to the tasks the users perform and should be highly intuitive. Visuals should require minimal text to explain them, allowing the users to understand the point being made immediately.

Culture B

Members of Culture B, on the other hand, view knowledge as something that is useless for the individual, unless it advances the group. This knowledge comes from external, highly respected sources, and the individual should memorize and keep this knowledge at hand.

A major cultural error is to advance the self over the group, and the individual who has personal goals and ambitions that do not come from those that the culture prescribes risks being excluded from that culture. Likewise, individuals are not expected to generate knowledge based on what education and experience presents. Rather, they are to use their memorized knowledge when using the product. Likewise, the culture does not reward those who violate this view. This culture frequently resists changes to procedures (such as the need to learn an updated version of the product), so change is rare. Once users in this culture have understood how the product will benefit the group—how it will fit in with other products—they want to keep on using it regardless of possible improvements in an updated version, unless they are told to do so and can understand how the revision will benefit the group.

For users in this culture, the communicator should stress the sources of the knowledge (emphasizing, for example, the reliability of the knowledge). Where does "credibility" come from for users in this culture? One possible source could be the realism of the examples. These should reflect both the tasks that the user is to perform and the culture of the user. The author should explain the examples, especially the visuals, so that there is no doubt as to the relevance and importance of the examples. If the examples stress group success, all the better. Also, if the examples remain consistent from product version to product version, the user will feel more comfortable should a new version appear and be approved for use.

Attitude Toward Education

Culture A

In this culture, education is assumed to be open to any who desire it. There are no cultural restrictions placed on who has access to it.

Anyone with the personal drive and determination can take advantage of numerous educational opportunities. If financing is a problem, various loans and scholarships are available to the student. The cultural attitude encourages people to pursue educational goals and rewards them for their efforts. Once the students complete their basic education, teachers and family encourage them to advance as far as possible because of the rewards waiting for the educated person— good job, good home, good life.

Education comes in a normal sequencing of events—there is a time and place for it in the general scheme of life. If an individual does not take advantage of the opportunities in the normal course of events, that person can do so later, although it is more desirable (from the culture's view) that education follow the chronological sequencing of life's events. The cultural attitude is such that members of the culture receive encouragement from a very early age (through role playing, toys, parental guidance, and so forth) to identify specific goals and objectives. While the culture does not necessarily discourage aimless pursuit of education for its own sake, it does reward those with definite goals and objectives.

Teachers are viewed as means to the end and are thought to be accountable for helping students achieve their goals and objectives and for fulfilling their needs. To teach is to assist in learning. The students facilitate their own learning by extrapolating materials (provided by the teachers—lectures, for example), and teachers guide and help the students in these tasks. For users in this culture, the communicator should emphasize learning how to use the product.

Culture B

By contrast, in *Culture B* education is considered a privilege and is open only to those in certain social classes. This culture also encourages personal goals and objectives, but is not as nearly insistent on them as is *Culture A*. Hypothetical *Culture B* sees extended education as being needed only by a select few of the privileged few and then as applied to promote the group rather than as a path for improving one's social position. All individuals are not encouraged to seek it, and culturally defined success is possible without it. It is possible for someone who is not of the privileged classes to take advantage of educational opportunities, but that person must be exceptionally strong to withstand the effects of not being in the privileged classes. Also, funds are usually not available for all who seek an extended education. Students, therefore, do not normally have strong individual goals and objectives toward which they work.

In *Culture B,* educational opportunities for those selected come in no particular sequence. The key cultural attitude is for the selected individual to be patient and wait for the opportunity. Likewise, unlike *Culture A,* the education is an end in itself and does not lead to other, specific ends. Because of these educational views, communicators will have difficulty establishing a style that will enhance the communication and not prevent the users from processing the text.

Teachers are normally venerated as sources of knowledge and wisdom. Failure of a student to reach an educational goal or objective or fulfill a need is viewed as not being the fault of the teacher but rather the student. Teachers provide materials (lectures, notes, readings, etc.) that students memorize. Rarely is the student asked to extrapolate from the source materials to personal application and understanding of the point being made.

For users in this culture, the communicator should emphasize the tasks and how these tasks relate to the overall operation of the program. The style should facilitate memorizing text. Examples should not rely on being intuitive; rather, lengthy explanations relating the example to the overall product and the culture's goals should be the norm.

Attitude Toward Products

Culture A

Products produced in *Culture A* are considered to be means to an end. Individuals should use them to reach individual goals and objectives, enhancing the self-reliance that the group cherishes and encourages. Ownership of products is parallel with social recognition and success because students completing an extended education receive more money for their work, thus enabling them to buy more products. They also do not hesitate to buy products to enhance their moving toward their goals.

The cultural attitude toward products is one that encourages the individual to find out what is the best product or tool to accomplish a personal goal and then use it ("Improve your productivity by buying this new PDA"). For cultures that understand the benefits of using the product, the communicator can minimize that aspect in the documentation.

For users in this culture, the communicator should emphasize the value of the product to the user and the user's goals and objectives as well as how much more efficient the product will make the user (hence, leading to positive rewards from the cultural group).

Culture B

All products in *Culture B* have a singular purpose—to help the group advance. As long as the product is helping the group, it is kept and used—even though newer products or newer versions of the product may be available. Change occurs only when the product no longer is perceived as helping the group.

If the products enhance only the individual, they are not endorsed. Because the culture discourages ownership for the sake of ownership or as a visible sign of success, products do not play a large part in an individual's standing in the group.

Decisions about products are frequently imposed on the group from the authoritative leadership. Presumably, that leadership carefully studies the product to make certain that it will benefit the group, and once established, the product typically will not be changed.

For users in this culture, the communicator should emphasize the benefits that the product offers the group ("This new PDA allows you to coordinate more easily within and outside your work group").

Attitude Toward Needs and Goals

The attitudes a culture has toward the individual's needs and goals summarizes that culture's subjective attitudes in general.

Culture A

This culture encourages individual and personal goals and objectives that will benefit and advance the individual. As individuals improve and advance, so too will the culture. If the person does not know something, that person is culturally encouraged to find out about it (e.g., it is not a cultural negative to ask for help). From acquiring an extended education to acquiring the goods and products of the society, these individuals are focused more on themselves than on the advancement of any group.

For users in this culture, the communicator should emphasize the actions and goals of the user and how the product accomplishes them.

Culture B

This culture, by contrast, discourages the individual in favor of the group. Individuals are not expected to have personal needs and goals that differ from the group's. Should individuals need information, they are actively discouraged from openly seeking it. They are expected to know what they need to know to advance the group. If they do need something, they are expected to find it quietly.

For users in this culture, the communicator should emphasize the value of the product to fulfilling the group's needs and goals. Examples should be group-oriented, as should all explanations of the examples.

In summary, then, the communicators must consider a number of factors when designing manuals for cross-cultural communication. For example,

- The type of group (does it stress individualism or the group?)
- The approach the user takes to the task (get right to work or acquire an overview of the manual before beginning?)
- The user's relationship to the language of the manual (a first, second, or even third language and what level of syntactical complexity?)

Developing a Manual

Manuals written for these two hypothetical cultures would be quite different. For *Culture A,* the manual's introduction would emphasize the progress of the individual and stress the importance of the product for that person's success. It would be written in a style that assumes some higher levels of formal education than might be assumed in *Culture B.* The logic of the document would follow a more Western approach, meaning that it would be chronological to a point, but would assume that the user will read the manual when having a problem.

The introduction for *Culture B* would stress that the product was important for the group's success, and the benefits of the product, including benefits of fulfilling each task, would be phrased in terms of the group rather than the individual. The communicator would have to "prove" the worth of the knowledge contained in the document, relying on the reputation and age of the company, for example. In addition, the style would be simpler, assuming that the user had less formal education than a user in *Culture A*. The logic of the document would depend on the chronological flow of the tasks, meaning that it would be organized differently. Throughout the manual, the examples should emphasize how performing a task in a particular way would enhance the group and help lead it to its goals.

A statement such as the following would be more appropriate for a user in *Culture B* than in *Culture A:* "Show the company's profit margin to best advantage by adjusting the size of the bars in the bar chart." To make a similar point for a user in *Culture A,* the statement could read, "To show the company's profit margin to best advantage, adjust the size of the bars in the bar chart."

Both manuals would have a different organization as well as style, all based on the cultural analysis. What follows is an example of such a manual and the problems of organizing it for *Culture A* and *Culture B.*[1]

ORGANIZING FOR THE TWO CULTURES

How would culture influence the way that the communicator would organize a technical manual? For example, a simple manual for using a graphics program and containing four sections would be organized differently for *Culture A* than for *Culture B*. The manual in this example is for a single software product.[2] The main sections of that manual are as follows:

- *Getting Started* (Brief Tutorial, General Information about the Program, Keyboard Conventions)
- *Frequently Asked Questions about the Program* (FAQ)
- *Using the Program* (Main Menu, Entering Data, Drawing Graphs, Saving to Disk, Advanced Features)
- *Technical Information about the Program and Specifications*

Table 1 shows how a communicator might organize the manual's sections for the two hypothetical cultures. What is the rationale for the different organization?

Users in *Culture A* want to get started immediately to improve their productivity. Therefore, the instructions will be more self-contained and task-oriented, rarely stressing how the task relates to the overall

[1] Chapter 6 has an extended analysis of an introduction for a software manual.
[2] For a more detailed explanation of this example, see Chapter 3.

Table 1. Organizing the Manual for Cultures A and B

Section	1st	2nd	3rd	4th
Culture A				
Getting Started				✔
Using the Program	✔			
FAQ		✔		
Technical Information			✔	
Culture B				
Getting Started		✔		
Using the Program			✔	
FAQ				✔
Technical Information	✔			

goal of the program: "To do this, do that" type of instructions. The communicator should focus on the user completing the tasks to achieve the job's needs and goals. Once users have understood how to use the program (assuming that they actually read the manual and do not depend on the intuitive nature of the program), the rest of the document is reference. Possibly, the user will not use any of the manual sections, but rely on whatever online help is available with the program. Communicators of documents for *Culture A* face a significant problem with the attitude of the members of this culture toward documentation.

Users in *Culture B* want all the information they can obtain before using the program. That information will stress how the user can enhance the total productivity of the group, meaning that each section would place an operation into the context of the overall purpose of the program: "Doing this task contributes to the final outcome in this way" would be a good approach. The communicator should focus on the user completing the tasks to fulfill the group's needs and goals.

CONCLUSION

In conclusion, then, cultural considerations should be as much a part of designing a manual as are other factors—target group analysis, task analysis, and translation/localization. Too often, however, the cultural elements are ignored because of time and budget difficulties, with the consequence that the manual does not fulfill its purpose of providing the user with the needed information.

The attitudes of a culture are significant factors for the communicator to consider when preparing a manual. Each attitude has implications for style, content, and organization. Communicators should consider the cultural implications their users bring to the document, as they consider what the user knows and does not know, can do and cannot do.

REFERENCES

1. A. N. Prior and others, History of Logic, in *The Encyclopedia of Philosophy*, P. Edwards (ed.), vol. IV. Macmillan Publishing Co., New York, pp. 513-571, 1967.
2. G. Hofstede, *Cultures and Organizations: Software of the Mind*, McGraw-Hill Book Company, New York, 1991.
3. G. Hofstede, Cultural Predictors of National Negotiation Styles, in *Processes of International Negotiation*, F. Mautner-Markhof (ed.), Westview Press, Boulder, Colorado, pp. 193-201, 1989.
4. G. Hofstede, *Culture's Consequences: International Differences in Work-Related Values*, Sage, Beverly Hills, California, 1987.
5. T. L. Warren, Three Approaches to Reader Analysis, *Technical Communication, 40*, pp. 81-88, 1993.

CHAPTER 6

Increasing User Acceptance of Technical information in Cross-Cultural Communication

Technical communication has as its primary rhetorical objective persuading users that the materials presented are accurate, instructive, and useful as well as possibly changing users' attitudes, behavior, or both while helping them meet their information needs. Gaining compliance with this rhetorical objective in the communication situation requires that technical communicators develop persuasive documents using the best tools from communication theory, rhetoric, and documentation processes (e.g., cultural user analysis). But which of the many theories of communication, which of the many rhetorical strategies, and which cultural elements should technical communicators select?

Technical communicators develop documents that change users' behavior (e.g., instructions), attitude (e.g., proposals), or both (e.g., recommendation reports). Therefore, it is important for them to understand how to increase the users' acceptance of the documents, and the firmer that acceptance, the more the communication accomplishes its purpose. But how to adapt the text to increase that acceptance is crucial for the authors.

One problem facing technical communicators who write instructions is that the actual step in the instruction (*Place tab B in slot A*) is almost completely neutral when analyzed by communication and rhetorical theories and by cultural analysis. Putting aside issues raised in translation (does Arabic, for example, have an equivalent verb for the English imperative verb form that does not culturally insult the user), communicators writing for users whose second (or third) language is English are left with adapting the text surrounding the actual steps. Thus, they must turn to introductions, overviews, context-setting paragraphs, and other similar, noninstructional text to establish an atmosphere that leads to user acceptance. These are the areas where communicators can apply communication, rhetorical, and cultural theories most effectively.

When the technical communicator develops a set of instructions, for example, the traditional requirements for each section suggest a rhetorical strategy to follow: *introduction:* use overviews; descriptions of objects; process description of steps; list of parts, tools, and equipment; and so on; *steps:* division/classification, narrative, and illustrations/examples (verbal and visual); and *troubleshooting:* cause-effect analysis. However, the communication theory approach to take for each section and the cultural elements to analyze are not so obvious. This chapter, therefore, discusses the three areas technical communicators should address when their primary purpose is to persuade the users for whom English is not their native language to modify behavior: communication, rhetorical, and cultural theories. The three sets of theories offer the communicator a number of possible strategies to persuade the users of the value of the materials.

COMMUNICATION THEORIES

Communication theories address many communication issues that are relevant for technical communicators. For example, one can view communication as a "system" and apply systems theory to generating successful documents (including information theory [Shannon and Weaver], cybernetics [Wiener], and General Systems Theory [von Bertalanffy]) [1]. Technical communicators, likewise, could rely on theories of signs, symbols, and language to develop documents that contain the meaning that users can understand (e.g., Peirce's classical semantic theory, Langer's theories of signs and symbols, or Chomsky's theories of generative grammar) [2].

Theories also abound that relate to message production—how technical communicators generate messages while writing—including cognitive theories such as constructivism (Delia and colleagues) and message design logic (O'Keefe) [3]. Or, technical communicators could concentrate on theories that explain how messages are understood. In this area, there are theories of meaning (Osgood), attribution (Heider), information integration (Fishbein's Expectancy-Value Theory), consistency (cognitive dissonance [Festinger]), judgment (social judgment [Sherif and colleagues] and elaboration likelihood [Petty and Cacioppo]) [4].

Many communication theories, therefore, can help technical communicators understand strategies for adapting text to the users' particular needs. For example, understanding constructionist theories (Delia, in [3]) of meaning development can help technical communicators make sure that the user's meanings and theirs are in accord. Technical communicators can imagine the schema development in the mind of the user, knowing that, as the theory suggests, reality is filtered by the way a person sees things—the constructs created in the user's mind. Thus, technical communicators could use Constructionist Theory to have the user perform a certain action relative to installing a device. By identifying the communication strategy or strategies that will best fit the user's capacity to process content and form and comply, they can increase the user's acceptance of the message.

Compliance means, quite simply, getting someone to do what you want them to do. How do you accomplish that task? For example, how do you get someone to bring you a cup of coffee? Or get your boss to commit more resources to your project? Or get your son or daughter to agree to a curfew? In all three cases, you could do any of several things individually or in combination:

- Be nice to the person before asking for compliance.
- Promise to return the favor.
- Remind the person of a debt (moral, social, monetary).
- Suggest that complying would have benefits for them such as a boost to their self-esteem.
- Suggest that the immediate environment would improve.
- Get angry for noncompliance.
- Threaten consequences.
- Lay a little guilt.
- Warn of serious consequences.
- Suggest compliance as an act of kindness toward the asker.
- Ask directly.
- Drop a hint or two.
- Lie about consequences.

While most theories for creating and understanding messages developed in oral communication research, technical communicators can apply many of them to their situations and improve both developing written texts and enhancing the way the user receives, understands, and accepts them.

Compliance addresses issues related to the user changing behavioral patterns and not the recipient changing an attitude. Compliance "does not require the target to agree with the advocacy—just simply perform the behavior" [5]. We want our users to follow the instructions that we give them rather than evaluating their attitudes toward the text, the technical communicator, the product, or the situation. Likewise, we are not usually interested in changing the reader's cognitive structures. If the reaction is something like, "I'll do it, but I won't like it," then we have achieved the basic purpose of modifying behavior rather than attitude. Yet, this behavioral change does not free technical communicators from adopting the most effective persuasive strategies when producing the document so as not to receive a negative reaction toward compliance. For example, when the government produces instructions for paying taxes, their primary rhetorical purpose is to get you to pay what you owe. They would like you to develop a positive attitude toward paying taxes, but this change of attitude is not one of their main rhetorical purposes in the instructions.

Because of how a technical communicator controls composing and wants to control how users receive messages, one especially useful theory of message production is Marwell and Schmitt's Compliance-Gaining Theory, one of a group of theories involving exchanging one thing for another, such as being successful in completing the instructions in exchange for explicitly following the text [6]. This theory suggests that communicators can gain compliance from the receivers of their messages by employing certain strategies when generating the messages. Marwell and Schmitt developed 16 strategies to use to gain compliance from the receiver of a message. (See Table 1 for a listing of those strategies and what they involve.) Because 16 is a large number of strategies and they often overlap, Marwell and Schmitt reduced them to 5 clusters of tactics:[1]

---

[1] In the listing that follows, I have modified Marwell and Schmitt's descriptions slightly by adding technical communicator and user and recasting the rest of the description.

- *Rewarding:* In this strategy, the technical communicator promises the user that if the user wants to be a success, then follow
  these instructions.
- *Punishing:* The technical communicator threatens that the user
  will be punished for not complying with the instruction. If the
  user does not follow the instruction in a particular way, then
  the user will fail at the task.
- *Expertise:* The technical communicator makes clear that he or
  she is the expert and the user is not. The technical communicator
  "knows" that it is best for the user to comply with the instruction
  to complete the task.
- *Impersonal Commitments:* The technical communicator relies
  on moral grounds to gain user compliance. For example, the
  culture may emphasize the individual or the group, and the
  technical communicator likewise emphasizes the appropriate
  cultural view. The user will feel good about complying and bad
  about noncompliance.
- *Personal Commitments:* The technical communicator relies on
  debt that the user owes to gain user compliance. The user "owes"
  the technical communicator compliance because of a previous
  incident (e.g., success on a preceding step) (Marwell and Schmitt
  in [6]).

RHETORICAL THEORIES

One of the oldest conscious strategies (or ways to develop a document or speech) used to communicate is rhetoric. All phases of
communication offer the communicators an opportunity to apply
particular rhetorical strategies to gain their objectives. Students
apply rhetorical strategies to term papers, oral presentations,
research reports, and so forth, and in technical communication, all
genres are open to rhetorical strategies. Thus, the communicator
should again analyze context and receivers and then select an appropriate approach [7].

Most people understand rhetoric to be a tool used to make a
communication more effective, with special emphasis on persuasion.
The one with the message rhetorically shapes the message to make
the communication cycle complete (create, send, receive, provide
feedback). That shaping points to the methods available to persuade,
and students learn to match the requirements to be persuasive with

Table 1. Marwell and Schmitt's 16 Compliance-Gaining Strategies

Strategy	Example
Promising	Promising a reward for compliance
Threatening	Indicating that punishment will be applied for noncompliance
Showing expertise about positive outcomes	Showing how good things will happen to those who comply
Showing expertise about negative outcomes	Showing how bad things will happen to those who do not comply
Liking	Displaying friendliness
Pregiving	Giving a reward before asking for compliance
Applying aversive stimulation	Applying punishment until compliance is received
Calling in a debt	Saying the person owes something for past favors
Making moral appeals	Describing compliance as the morally right thing to do
Attributing positive feelings	Telling the other person how good he or she will feel if there is compliance
Attributing negative feelings	Telling the other person how bad he or she will feel if there is noncompliance
Positive altercasting	Associating compliance with people with good qualities
Negative altercasting	Associating noncompliance with people with bad qualities
Seeking altruistic compliance	Seeking compliance simply as a favor
Showing positive esteem	Saying that the person will be more liked by others if he or she complies

Source: Adapted from Marwell and Schmitt [6].

the means of doing so. Consequently, contemporary rhetoric has focused on different modes of development one can use to persuade (see Table 2 for a listing of the modes and their uses).

Another element in modern rhetoric is looking at the author's motives (see, for example, Kenneth Burke's *A Grammar of Motives*

Table 2. Rhetorical Strategies and Their Uses

Strategy	Interpretation	Application
Description	To detail what a person, place, or object is like	Here is what the product looks like
Narration	To relate an event	Sequence of steps
Illustration	To provide specific instances or examples	Verbal/visual presentations of concepts
Division-classification	To divide something into parts or to group related things in categories	Divide the assembly into steps/parts. Does the reader need to see the relationship of the whole to the parts?
Process analysis	To explain how something happens or how something is done	Overview of process
Comparison-contrast	To point out similarities and/or dissimilarities	Compare solutions. Does the reader need to have a variety of choices? In one culture (authoritative), one answer; in another, multiple answers to same problem, and reader selects?
Cause-effect	To analyze reasons and consequences	Sequences leading to solution? For reader, depends on system of logic culture teaches?
Definition	To explain the meaning of a term or concept	Explain terms/concepts. Culture assumes that reader already knows terms/concepts? *Face* in asking for help?

Source: Adapted from Nadell [7, pp. 30-32, 46].

and a Rhetoric of Motives and speech-act theory [8]). Why does the author want to change the attitude, behavior, or both, of the receivers? Based on that motive, the author selects a particular rhetorical approach to develop the document. With the actual instruction itself being relatively rhetoric-free, the author must turn, as I mentioned above, to the surrounding text to accomplish the rhetorical purpose.

USING COMMUNICATION AND RHETORICAL THEORIES

Preparing to Communicate

Compliance-Gaining (C-G) theory offers technical communicators a series of strategies that they can use to enhance the text and increase the user's acceptance of the material. Using C-G can be of special benefit when the technical communicators must consider that the user will use the document in a cross-cultural situation. Normally, communicators would develop documents meant for use across cultures by preparing a basic language version of the document, translating it into the target language, and then localizing it for cultural issues. Many companies, however, cannot afford this costly and time-consuming process, and so must rely on their technical communicators to produce documents that users in other cultures can accept—especially if the document is written in English and the user has English as a second or third language.

Selecting Rhetorical Strategies

By themselves, especially when considering written documents, C-G strategies can lack effectiveness because of most users' resistance to overt pressure, regardless of cultural background. Technical communicators must employ other strategies to make their communications useful and acceptable for users. One of these strategies is rhetorical, including different approaches to presenting the material, such as description, narration, illustration, division-classification, process analysis, comparison-contrast, cause-effect, and definition (see Table 2).

The need to persuade leads the technical communicator to select an appropriate way to present the materials based on reader analysis. Would the reader be more receptive to the material if it were presented as a description or a definition or within a narrative, or some other form? The key is identifying what makes the material more acceptable to the reader. Each of the approaches addresses a particular concern that the reader has about the information. In instructions, the preferred approach is chronological, where one step should follow another. But what about the material surrounding the actual steps? What is the best approach to use to present it so that it is acceptable to the reader?

INCLUDING CULTURAL ANALYSIS

This brings us to the third element in developing documentation that persuades the user that the material is useful, accurate, and meaningful: cultural analysis. In analyzing the user's culture, the technical communicator considers many factors such as demographic information about the users, the users' organizational roles, and the users' psychological profile [9].

As I have discussed previously (Chapter 5), one cause of unread, unused, and misunderstood manuals is the author's failure to consider culture—all the objective and subjective elements the author must consider when developing a document. If the author does not consider both sets of elements, resistance to the text will be strong—at both a conscious and subconscious level. Therefore, the author should do more than the obvious analysis of the reader based on objective elements.

Of the many subjective cultural elements that technical communicators must consider, one of the most important is the attitude of the culture toward the individual. For the purposes of this chapter, I will assume two hypothetical cultures, A and B (for more on these two hypothetical cultures, see Chapter 5).

Culture A emphasizes that the individual is important by sanctioning individual goals, aspirations, and ambitions. The culture rewards the individual who is driven toward goals. Individuals in this culture develop a strong sense of personal success—whether at the level of the individual instruction or the overall task itself.

The implications for the technical communicator, then, are to use strategies that will heighten the individual sense of accomplishment, leading to rewards. Technical communicators can focus on the individual by using second-person *you* as a singular pronoun and, where appropriate, first-person *I* referring to the user. The strategy is that success will come to the individual on the basis of a particular instruction as well as the cumulative effect of success in completing the task.

In hypothetical *Culture B,* the individual is de-emphasized in favor of the group. Individual goals and ambitions are subsumed under those of the group, and the culture emphasizes the group; the success of the individual is deprecated. Individuals in this culture develop a strong sense of group success—whether at the level of the individual instruction or the overall task itself.

The implications for technical communicators writing for individuals in this culture are to de-emphasize individual achievement and emphasize instead how the group will succeed. Pronouns should be third person, plural *they* (or *you* as a plural) and should stress benefits to the group. Success will come to the group not on the basis of a particular instruction but based on the cumulative effect of success in completing the task.

Applying Strategies

Table 3 shows examples of how we can combine compliance-gaining and rhetorical strategies and their outcome in the two hypothetical cultures—of course, many other combinations are possible. But which strategy (or strategies) should the author apply to the instructions? A 1991 study by Sullivan and Taylor [10] points out that when American and Japanese managers were devising strategies to gain compliance, they assumed the strategies should include reasoning and friendliness. However, traditional Japanese managerial style relied on loyalty and a sense of obligation to achieve organizational goals. As Sullivan and Taylor discovered, loyalty and obligations to company goals depend on employment for life at both the managerial and worker levels. In companies where such an employment policy was not in effect, other strategies had to be used to gain employees' compliance.

Their study suggests that managers (Japanese) use reasoning more often than assertiveness, depending on loyalty, and so forth. What the study further suggests is that when writing warnings, cautions, and the like (other than for dangerous circumstances) in instructions, authors should rely on reasoning to get their message across and accepted by the reader—providing explanations to support requests and stating the objective merits of the request.

Table 3. Summary of Strategies and Implications for Two Cultures

Compliance-Gaining	Suggested Rhetorical Strategy	Impact on Cultures A and B
Rewarding	Cause-effect	A: You will be rewarded B: The group will benefit
Punishing	Description	A: You will fail B: The group will fail
Expertise	Comparison-contrast	A: I've been there; done that B: I've seen impact on group productivity
Impersonal commitments; moral duty	Process	A: You will accomplish tasks B: The group will meet goals
Personal commitments; owe a debt	Process	A: Owe it to yourself B: Owe it to the group

Compliance is as important for instructions as it is as a management tool. The user must comply with the instructions to complete the task satisfactorily. And the best strategy to use (whether communication or rhetorical theories or cultural analysis) depends on how the technical communicator perceives the situation. If writing for a Japanese audience that is not permanently employed, appeals to loyalty will not work. On the other hand, the technical communicator who uses a C-G strategy focused on the cultural attitude toward the individual could find greater acceptance of the instructions.

To see how the prose surrounding the actual instructions can reflect all three theories, I examined the opening paragraph from a software manual. The specific example is aimed more at an individual from *Culture A* than *Culture B,* yet the way the technical communicator applied all three theories can be instructive.

Sample for Analysis: Microsoft Office 2000

When you acquire Microsoft Office 2000, you receive the manual *Discovering Microsoft Office 2000: Premium and Professional* [11].

This manual provides an introduction to the software and chapters on its components. An Appendix describes features for persons with disabilities. Judging from the tone of Chapter 1 ("Introducing Microsoft Office 2000"), the company's rhetorical goal is to make readers glad that they have the product. They want to persuade readers that this product will fulfill all their needs, making them highly productive workers.

Section one ("Welcome to Office 2000") opens with the following paragraph:

> Microsoft® Office 2000 office suite opens an exciting new door to business computing for the millennium. Now you can work faster and more efficiently than ever before by using the wealth of new features that Office 2000 provides. That much you might expect. But Office 2000 also offers new ways to collaborate with other people who are using the Web, or with your company's intranet. Whether you work with people in the same room, down the hall, or around the world, Office 2000 can help you in ways that you might not imagine.

The section, after this opening paragraph, goes on to explain the features of the book (the manual) and who are the assumed users of the product. I want to take a close look at this opening paragraph, with a special focus on the strategies we can infer from it. Table 4 summarizes this analysis

What does the analysis show? The main C-G strategy is rewards and promises based on expertise: "Do what we tell you to do and you will succeed." Paired with this strategy is the rhetorical strategy of description—describing that success. Finally, the cultural strategy is to focus on individual rewards (*you* singular) even when describing how collaboration with others will be successful now that you are using the product. The paragraph, therefore, was directed to a reader from *Culture A*.

Changing the paragraph to focus on a reader from *Culture B* would mean broadening the application of the rewards promised to include the group (*you* plural; better would be *your work group*). Using promises and rewards as C-G strategies, coming from a position of expertise would be appropriate, as would the rhetorical strategy of description.

Before making such a change, however, the author should consider the findings of Sullivan and Taylor's research, dated though they may be. In their study, no specific C-G strategy as identified by them

Table 4. Analysis of Sample Paragraph

Sentence	C-G strategy	Rhetorical strategy	Cultural strategy
Microsoft® Office 2000 office suite opens an exciting new door to business computing for the millennium.	Expertise ("I" know . . .) to support promise.	Description—definitive action *opens*.	Looks outward to *business*.
Now you can work faster and more efficiently than ever before by using the wealth of new features that Office 2000 provides.	Reward: promise of results from complying.	Description of what will happen.	Individual benefits—*you*.
That much you might expect.	Expertise: "I" understand you.	Cause-effect— benefits → expectation.	Uses second-person *you*, individual goals and expectations.
But Office 2000 also offers new ways to collaborate with other people who are using the Web, or with your company's intranet.	Reward: comply and get additional collaboration.	Comparison-contrast between old and new ways of working	Working with others. But still uses second-person *your*.
Whether you work with people in the same room, down the hall, or around the world, Office 2000 can help you in ways that you might not imagine.	Expertise: "I" know what will happen.	Narration: presents "story."	Encourages improved work within the group. But still uses second-person *you*.

was needed. Rather, C-G came through using polite frankness. Sullivan and Taylor discovered that an appeal to loyalty only worked when both the manager and worker were permanently employed. That situation of permanent employment is changing, so different approaches to gaining compliance as well as rhetorical and cultural strategies need to be discovered.

CONCLUSION

Communication theory offers a wide range of approaches that authors can adopt; so, too, does rhetorical and cultural analysis theory. When authors prepare instructions, they want to modify the behavior of their readers (rather than modifying their attitudes) so that the readers accept the accuracy and validity of the instructions. Lead-in and follow-up materials, however, can be developed using all three theories.

As I have shown in this chapter, authors of documents meant for readers whose native language is not English and whose companies cannot justify the cost of professional localization can prepare their documents by being aware of and applying strategies when they prepare their documents. Three such strategies are compliance-gaining, rhetorical, and cultural analysis. Authors can use all three to persuade their readers to accept the document's contents by understanding the objective and subjective cultural elements involved in any cross-cultural communication.

REFERENCES

1. See, for example, C. Shannon and W. Weaver, *The Mathematical Theory of Communication,* University of Illinois Press, Urbana, 1949; N. Wiener, *Cybernetics or Control and Communication in the Animal and the Machine,* MIT Press, Cambridge, 1961; also Wiener's *The Human Use of Human Beings: Cybernetics and Society,* Houghton Mifflin, Boston, 1954; and L. von Bertalanffy, General Systems Theory: A Critical Review, *General Systems, 7,* pp. 1-20, 1962; and Bertalanffy's *General Systems Theory: Foundations, Development, Applications,* Braziller, New York, 1968.
2. See, for example, C. S. Peirce, *Charles S. Peirce: Selected Writings,* P. O. Wiener (ed.), Dover, New York, 1958; S. Langer, *Mind: An Essay on Human Feeling,* 3 vols., Johns Hopkins University Press, Baltimore, 1967, 1972; also Langer's *Philosophy in a New Key,* Harvard University Press, Cambridge, 1942; N. Chomsky, Three Models for the Description

of Language, *Transactions on Information Theory,* IT-2, pp. 113-124, 1956; also Chomsky's *Studies on Semantics in Generative Grammar,* Mouton, The Hague, 1972.

3. See, for example, J. G. Delia, B. J. O'Keefe, and D. J. O'Keefe, The Constructivist Approach to Communication, in *Human Communication Theory: Comparative Essays,* F. E. X. Dance (ed.), Harper & Row, New York, pp. 147-191, 1982; and B. O'Keefe, Variation, Adaptation, and Functional Explanation in the Study of Message Design, in *Developing Communication Theories,* G. Philipsen (ed.), SUNY Press, Albany, pp. 85-118, 1997.

4. C. Osgood, *Cross Cultural Universals of Affective Meaning,* University of Illinois Press, Urbana, 1975; also Osgood's The Nature and Measurement of Meaning, in *The Semantic Differential Technique,* J. Snider and C. Osgood (eds.), Aldine, Chicago, pp. 9-10, 1969; F. Heider, *The Psychology of Interpersonal Relations,* Wiley, New York, 1958; M. Fishbein and I. Ajzen, *Belief, Attitude, Intention, and Behavior,* Addison-Wesley, Reading, Massachusetts, 1975; L. Festinger, *A Theory of Cognitive Dissonance,* Stanford University Press, Stanford, 1957; L. Festinger and J. M. Carlsmith, Cognitive Consequences of Forced Compliance, *Journal of Abnormal and Social Psychology, 58,* pp. 203-210, 1959; M. Sherif, C. Sherif, and R. Nebergall, *Attitude and Attitude Change: The Social Judgment Involvement Approach,* Saunders, Philadelphia, 1965; and R. E. Petty and J. T. Cacioppo, *Communication and Persuasion: Central and Peripheral Routes to Attitude Change,* Springer-Verlag, New York, 1986.

5. K. Rhoads, Working Psychology: Definitions—Compliance, www.workingpsychology.com/definit.html (accessed May 4, 2005).

6. G. Marwell and D. R. Schmitt, Dimensions of Compliance-Gaining Strategies: A Dimensional Analysis, *Sociometry, 30,* pp. 350-364, 1967. For an analysis of the theory, see L. R. Wheeless, R. Barraclough, and R. Stewart, Compliance-Gaining and Power in Persuasion, in *Communication Yearbook 7,* R. N. Bostrom (ed.), Sage, Beverly Hills, California, pp. 105-145, 1983; R. L. Wiseman and W. J. Schenck-Hamlin, A Multidimensional Scaling Validation of an Inductively-Derived Set of Compliance-Gaining Strategies, *Communication Monographs, 48*:4, pp. 251-270, 1981; W. J. Schenck-Hamlin and others, A Model of Properties of Compliance-Gaining Strategies, *Communication Quarterly, 30*:2, pp. 92-100, 1982; M. G. Garko, Perspectives on and Conceptualizations of Compliance, and Compliance-Gaining, *Communication Quarterly, 38,* pp. 138-157, 1990; S. A. Hellweg and others, An Analysis of Compliance-Gaining Instrumentation in the Organizational Communication Literature, *Management Communication Quarterly, 4,* pp. 244-271, 1990; J. J. Sullivan, A Cross-Cultural Test of Compliance-Gaining Theory, *Management Communication Quarterly, 5,* pp. 220-239, 1991.

7. See, for example, the rhetorical strategies described in J. Nadell and others, *The Macmillan Writer: Rhetoric, Reader, Handbook* (2nd Edition), Macmillan, New York, 1994.

8. K. Burke, *A Grammar of Motives and a Rhetoric of Motives,* Meridian Books, The World Publishing Company, Cleveland, 1945, 1952. For key texts in speech-act theory, see J. Searle, *Speech Acts: An Essay in the Philosophy of Language,* Cambridge University Press, Cambridge, 1969.

9. T. L. Warren, Three Approaches to Reader Analysis, *Technical Communication, 40,* pp. 81-88, 1993.

10. J. Sullivan and S. Taylor, A Cross-Cultural Test of Compliance-Gaining Theory, *Management Communication Quarterly, 5,* pp. 220-239, 1991.

11. Microsoft Corporation, *Discovering Microsoft Office 2000: Premium and Professional,* Microsoft Corporation, Redmond, Washington, p. 2, 1999.

CHAPTER 7

Conclusion

Cross-cultural communication is now a fact of life for organizations that wish to broaden the market for their products or services. No longer can they assume that their documents will be read by a homogeneous or near-homogeneous audience based in the same culture as they are. Even within a specific country, there are cultural characteristics that influence how the audience will receive the documents and how much credibility they will place in them. Authors now must consider the audience's culture as well as the other areas that make up audience analysis—demographics, user profiles, role in an organization, psychological needs, and much more.

The problem is to identify just what a culture is. Can we associate it with a geopolitical boundary of some kind? A religion? A profession? All have a culture, but is it possible to include everything in that audience profile? Authors have to make choices, and those choices directly affect how they will adapt the document for different cultural groups.

Much of the work of making a document culturally sensitive falls to the translator and localizer. But this is expensive, time-consuming work, adding weeks and months to a schedule that is already packed and, in many cases, not really all that stable. And then the question of whether the organization can afford translation and localization imposes new problems for the documents. Very large organizations with large budgets and long lead times can manage the extra expense and time; small to medium-size organizations typically cannot. So, how can they make their documents more culturally aware to increase their being accepted and used by the audience?

This book has presented some suggestions on how authors can become aware of the cultural implications of their documents and what they can do to enhance their acceptance and use. Being culturally aware when drafting documents can go a long way to making the documents more useful and helping the audience keep the reading process at a subconscious level.

I began in Chapter 1 by outlining the problem and offering definitions of *culture*—a step, it seems to me, that has to happen before any adaptation of text can begin. When we look at a complex abstraction such as *culture*, it is easy to get lost in a long, convoluted attempt to define it. I chose to use a simpler approach by identifying culture as Limaye and Victor [1] have done: objective elements (laws, rules, codified behavior models, etc.) and subjective elements (noncodified behavior models and attitudes) offer a less complex way to approach *culture*. From there, the author can measure the quality of the document against these models and adapt the document if needed.

The author can also use various elements or tools to make the documents more acceptable. For example, the author can use communication and rhetorical theory (Chapter 6) to enhance the credibility of the documents; even the language (codes) that the author uses can form part of the writing strategies (Chapters 3 and 4); and the author can use metadiscourse in connection with other strategies to aid the audience (Chapters 4 and 6).

Cross-cultural communication problems are not restricted to companies because even in international standards development, style documents must be sensitive to cross-cultural issues (Chapter 4). Even the way you organize a document can be influenced by culture (Chapters 3 and 5). How does the audience want to receive information—big picture followed by details, or details followed by big picture, or, as the survey showed, a mixture of the two? That same survey offered some insight on how communicators think of culture. Tied to a country? Profession? Religion? And what do you consider when you know that you will be organizing a document for a cross-cultural situation (Chapter 3, Table 7)?

STRATEGIES FOR MAKING A "GOOD" CROSS-CULTURAL COMMUNICATION

Audience Analysis

Doing an effective audience analysis is where most authors begin. They develop profiles of the assumed readers of their documents based either on personal knowledge (a progress report intended specifically for an immediate supervisor) or on models (developing demographic, organizational, and psychological assumptions about readers not personally known—a vice-president, for example). Some companies even develop profiles of users of their products and services, and writers can draw on these for their audience analysis.

Based on these profiles, writers can adapt documents to enhance the reader's understanding of the information. They can adapt style, level of technical detail, organization, visuals (adapting or even adding), purpose, function, and other elements. An axiom in technical communication suggests that the better the audience analysis, the better the document.

But something is missing in these traditional audience analysis procedures found in textbooks, corporate style manuals, and the research: cultural elements are ignored beyond the surface levels—getting the vocabulary and visuals right, for example. Much more is involved in cultural analysis than these items—as I hope I have shown.

Cultural Analysis

Analyzing a culture begins by understanding what a *culture* is—how to define a culture. As the Bibliography and the Appendix show, a lot of material is available and a lot of assumptions are made about culture and what elements there are in a culture—especially what elements a writer should be concerned about when producing documents.

Certainly, the same elements are found in cultural analysis that I mentioned above for audience analysis (demographics, for example). Each of them can influence the way the writer prepares the document, so that adapting one document for several cultures becomes a rather complex and complicated job.

Demographics as an Example

Demographics involve what you can ask about and measure. Going through the entire list of demographic elements would exceed the scope of this chapter and book, but I want to mention a few that can be significant when analyzing the demographics of a culture.

One of the easiest things to ask about (at least in Western cultures) is age and education. These two form the basis for adapting documents because (at least in Western cultures) knowing the educational level of the reader can have implications for style, level of technical detail, complexity of visuals and mathematics, and so forth. In Western cultures (at least in the United States), reading is cumulative in terms of the complexity of the materials. First-grade readers offer very short and simple sentences. The complexity of the sentences and the paragraphs increases until the student reaches late high school and on into college/university, when the sentences and paragraphs are highly complex. Presumably, the reader, having, for example, a university education, should be able to read comfortably material that is complex in presentation.

What about other cultures? Middle-Eastern, for example? How are their students taught to read? Can we assume that readers who have a university education have an accompanying high level of comfort with complex sentences and paragraphs. Added to this issue is the amount of education and practice the assumed reader has with English—the reader's second or even third language. When the native language can be assumed to be a Western language (German, Spanish, French, Italian, etc.), writers can make some limited assumptions about the relationship between education and reading skill. But what if the native language is Arabic or Chinese? What kinds of assumptions can writers make that allow them to adapt text? And a further problem is, does the reader know English from having learned U.K. English or Indian English or American English?

Matters can become even more complicated when the writer considers the role of the individual in an organization. The Appendix (p. 109) suggests that the traditional Western view of the individual within an organization differs substantially from that of someone from a traditional Eastern culture. Added to this mix is the culture's attitude toward the individual (see the hypothetical cultures described in Chapters 3 and 5). When the value of the individual falls second to the value of the group, how should the writer modify the way the information is presented?

Thus, developing an effective audience analysis profile, including cultural implications, is complex and complicated and, while time-consuming, should pay dividends in reader acceptance of the documents.

Communication Theory

It is impossible not to communicate—from the nonverbal elements of oral communication to the way a page is designed in a written text.

Many theories exist to explain how that transference of information occurs. Knowing how the communication works can help writers develop more effective documents. In this book, I have used two of the theories that I believe can make a difference when writers develop documents (Bernstein's Elaborated and Restricted Codes and Marwell and Schmitt's Compliance-Gaining). But there are others that can be equally effective. To date, there is no Ur-Theory or Grand Unification Communication Theory to turn to for answers on how best to present the materials. Until one arrives, writers should be familiar with the kinds of theories that are available and judiciously apply them to their work. The worst thing that can happen is for a writer to use a single approach regardless of the situation.

Rhetorical Theory

Unlike communication theory, rhetorical theory has a relatively uniform approach as well as a long and stable history as taught in high schools, colleges, and universities. Writers can draw on centuries of rhetorical strategies when creating documents. Originally, the suggested purpose of rhetoric was to persuade, but rhetoric has come to mean more a method of development that is selected based on the material, the receiver, and the purpose of the communication. Some methods are intuitive from the materials to be presented (chronological development used in a progress report), while some material may lend itself to one or more methods (a mechanism can be described, classified, divided, etc.).

These approaches are Western in history and practice. What are the rhetorical approaches used in Eastern or Middle-Eastern communication? Can we assume that a reader from a Middle-Eastern culture has the same rhetorical expectations and abilities to process material as does a reader from a Western culture? How do readers in different cultures view the data that writers use to develop their documents? What approach will persuade them of the material's importance or validity or the writer's credibility? Knowing something of the rhetorical traditions of different cultures can be as important as knowing how the subjective elements of a culture influence the document's reception [2].

Stylistic Aids—Metadiscourse

Finally, style. Style, a term as elusive to define as *quality* and *culture,* allows the author to enhance the meaning that a sentence or paragraph communicates. Arranging sentence and paragraph elements in different ways to enhance the document offers the author a chance to consider how the culture of the reader influences reading (overview first or last, Old Information first or last, for example). One of the major stylistic tools available to authors is metadiscourse. Yet, the materials referenced in Chapter 4 focus on using metadiscourse in a Western, English-language setting. But can we assume that the way metadiscourse works in a Western—specifically English-language—culture parallels in any way how metadiscourse works in another culture? With metadiscourse showing how the writer intends the reader to process the material, one might assume that processing would be the same across cultures. Yet, cultural attitudes (such as those discussed in Chapter 5) can be considerably different toward such matters as education, goals, the individual, and so forth.

Another aspect is the way that writers using the Western, English-language cultural traditions think about how to organize sentences—mainly Old Information (or context) followed by New Information (what the reader does not know). Is the same strategy viable in, say, a Hebrew-language culture or Japanese-language culture?

GUIDELINES AND RECOMMENDATIONS

From these views of cross-cultural communication, I want to offer some recommendations to communicators who will write in English for receivers whose first language is not English:

1. Shift your perspective. Realize that in this document you are creating, you are generating a new culture.
2. View yourself as an intercultural communicator. That is, broaden your views when you are preparing a document for another culture. Do a more detailed audience analysis and try to learn as much as you can about the receivers' culture. For example, how do the receivers in that culture reason and think? How do they process data? What to them is accepted as proof? What persuasive techniques work? What are their attitudes toward the product or service, the document, or even the author?
3. Develop an understanding of your own culture. What, exactly, do you know about your own culture? Is yours characterized by open-role, Elaborated Code, and so on? Or do some other

descriptions fit? How do you define your own culture? Something political? Religious? Geopolitical?

4. Be aware that the actual product or service that you are documenting can have cultural implications. As one respondent pointed out at FORUM95 (Chapter 3, Table 7), products carry a culture. The example product—a business graphing software product—might be designed to save the user time when the user's culture does not consider saving time as a benefit.

5. There is no substitute for a native speaker's review of the documents. But, if issues with time and cost are substantial enough to call such a service into question, then the other recommendations here are the options the author must consider.

REFERENCES

1. M. R. Limaye and D. A. Victor, Cross-Cultural Business Communication Research: State of the Art and Hypotheses for the 1990s, *Journal of Business Communication, 28,* pp. 277-299, 1991.
2. G. A. Kennedy, *A Comparative Rhetoric: An Historical and Cross-Cultural Introduction,* Oxford University Press, New York, 1998.

Appendix

AN OPPORTUNITY TO COMPARE VIEWS:
U.S. Culture vs. Traditional Eastern Culture
(Japan/China, for example) vs. a Target Culture

Item	U.S. *vs.* Traditional Eastern	Target Culture
Business relations	Competition *vs.* Harmony	
Orientation	Individual *vs.* Group	
Behavior	Diverse, few norms *vs.* Not unique, norms	
Identity	Individual *vs.* Family, group, company	
Relationships	Short-term *vs.* Long-term	
Approach	Quick to make friends; first name basis *vs.* Slow; formal address	
Strangers	Quick to acknowledge *vs.* Rare to acknowledge	
Anger	Acceptable *vs.* Unacceptable	
Communication		
Logic	Cause/effect reasoning *vs.* Logic of relation	
Silence	Avoid *vs.* Use	
Truth	Absolute *vs.* Relative	
Values	Based on religion *vs.* Based on feelings	
Mistakes	OK to admit *vs.* Never force another to admit to a mistake	
Criticism	Of action, not person; expected *vs.* None; unexpected; avoid	
Understanding	Ask for clarification *vs.* Do not admit not understanding	

Style	Direct and to the point; fast vs. Indirect; ambiguous; slow
Answers	Direct, even if negative vs. Politeness more important
Problems	Confront, solve quickly vs. Circumvent
Eye contact	Direct vs. Avoid direct; be indirect
Distance away from other	About 30 inches vs. More than 30 inches
Touching	Special friends, family vs. Dislike of all physical contact
Answering "Yes" means . . .	"I agree" vs. "I hear you"
Leadership/Status	
Authority	Independent, open to question vs. Dependent, do not question
Status	Power most important vs. Maturity (age) essential
Source of status	Personality, politics, vs. Family connections, titles, education, age
Debate	Like it vs. Dislike confrontation
Disagreements	OK, if not personal vs. Rude if direct and personal
Decisions (who can decide)	Individual vs. People in authority
Pace of environment	Quick vs. Slow
Input	OK from lower down vs. Top down
Loyalty	To self and career vs. To work unit

Appendix (Cont'd.)

Item	U.S. vs. Traditional Eastern	Target Culture
Productivity	Expected of all *vs.* Comes from working as a family	
Planning	Short-term *vs.* Long-term	
Meetings	Communication tool; all participate *vs.* Leader only speaks	
Atmosphere in meetings	Joking OK *vs.* Joking not OK	
Legal arrangements	Detailed *vs.* Prefer to be vague and then create specific as you go	
Legal contracts	Detailed contracts; inflexible *vs.* Vague contracts; flexible	
Discussion	All participate *vs.* No participation	
Adjourn when?	Time-driven *vs.* Business driven	
Decisions taken when?	At meetings *vs.* Before the meeting	
Bargaining	Grudgingly; no haggling *vs.* Expects to; wants concessions	
Who makes decisions?	Executives do not always make them *vs.* Made at highest levels	
Summary (among other points)	U.S.: Impatient Limited experiences Individual initiative Things move quickly	Traditional Eastern: Focus on relationships Dislike conflict Relationships important Use large teams	Target:

Communication Suggestions for
U.S. Readers/Listeners

1. Always include detailed summaries and overviews. Tell the reader where you are going and, in a long report, where you have been.
2. Build reports in two major sections: (A) General, meant for the nontechnical expect. Relatively short—5 to 10 pages at most (Executive Summary). (B) Highly technical for technical people. Relatively long.
3. Teamwork is important, but there are times when the individual must stand for a belief/view but be very certain of the "price" such a stance requires.
4. While there is a definite hierarchy on paper (the company organizational chart), interaction among levels is frequent and many times required (for fast action). Expect to use first names shortly after meeting.

Bibliography

This bibliography is preliminary and selective. Entries come from a variety of sources including the references found in articles on the topic.*

Accent on Internationalization: Guidelines for Software Internationalization. Boulder, CO: International Language Engineering (ILE), 1994.

Adler, Nancy J. "Cross-Cultural Management Research: The Ostrich and the Trend." *Academy of Management Review,* 8, no. 2 (1983): 226-232.

Adler, Nancy J., and J. L. Graham. "Cross-Cultural Interaction: The International Comparison Fallacy?" *Journal of International Business Studies,* 20, no. 3 (1989): 515-537.

Almaney, A. J., and A. J. Alwan. *Communicating with the Arabs: A Handbook for the Business Executive.* Prospect Heights, IL: Waveland Press, 1982.

Alred, Geof, Michael Fleming, and Michael Byram. *Intercultural Experience and Education.* Buffalo, NY: Multilingual Matters, 2003.

Alston, Jan P. *The Intelligent Businessman's Guide to Japan.* Rutland, VT: Charles T. Tuttle Co., 1990.

Andrews, Deborah, ed. *International Dimensions of Technical Communication.* Arlington, VA: Society for Technical Communication, 1995.

Arnold, Michael D. "Building a Truly World Wide Web: A Review of the Essentials of International Communication." *Technical Communication,* 45, no. 2 (1998): 197-206.

Asante, M. K., and W. B. Gudykunst, eds. *Handbook of International and Intercultural Communication.* Newbury Park, CA: Sage, 1989.

Axtell, Roger, E., rev. ed. *The Do's and Taboos of International Trade: A Small Business Primer.* New York: John Wiley & Sons, 1994.

Axtell, Roger E., ed. *Do's and Taboos Around the World,* 3rd ed. New York: John Wiley & Sons, 1993.

*Special thanks to Ph.D. students Candice McKee and Hui Zeng for their help on this bibliography.

Baldwin, John R., and Stephen K. Hunt. "Information-Seeking Behavior in Intercultural and Intergroup Communication." *Human Communication Research,* 28, no. 2 (2002): 272-287.

Banks, W. P., E. Oka, and S. Shugarman. "Recoding of Printed Words to Internal Speech: Does Recoding Come Before Lexical Access?" In *The Perception of Print: Reading Research in Experimental Psychology,* ed. Ovid J. L. Tzeng and Harry Singer. Hillsdale, NJ: Erlbaum, 1981.

Bargiela-Chiappin, Franesca and Catherine Nickerson. "Intercultural Business Communication: A Rich Field of Studies." *Journal of Intercultural Studies,* 24, no. 1 (2003): 3-15.

Barnlund, D. C. *Public and Private Self in Japan and the United States: Communicative Styles of Two Cultures.* Yarmouth, ME: International Press, 1975.

Barnum, Carol, et al. "Globalizing Technical Communication: A Field Report from China." *Technical Communication,* 48, no. 4 (2001): 397-420.

Baum, Nancy. "The Pleasures and Pratfalls of Editing for Foreign Writers," *FORUM 95: PostHarvest* (1985): 166-170.

Beck, B. E. F., and L. F. Moore. "Linking the Host Culture to Organizational Variables." In *Organizational Culture,* eds. Peter J. Frost, et al. Beverly Hills, CA: Sage, 1985, pp. 335-354.

Belloni, Maria Carman. "Social Time Dimensions as Indicators of Class Distinction in Italy." *International Social Science Journal,* 38, no. 1 (1986): 65-76.

Bernstein, Basil. *Class, Codes, and Control,* vol. I: *Theoretical Studies Toward a Sociology of Language.* 3 vols. London: Routledge and Kegan Paul, 1971.

Besner, D., and M. Coltheart. "Ideographic and Alphabetic Processing in Skilled Reading of English." *Neuropsychologia,* 17, no. 5 (1979): 467-472.

Biederman, Irving and Yao-Chung Tsao. "On Processing Chinese Ideographs and English Words: Some Implications from Stroop Test Results." *Cognitive Psychology,* 11, no. 2 (1979): 125-132.

Blicq, Ron, ed. *Guidelines for Writing English-Language Technical Documentation for an International Audience.* Winnipeg, Manitoba: INTECOM, 2003.

Bliss, C. K. "Semantography: One Writing for One World." In *Symbol Sourcebook,* ed. H. Dreyfuss. New York: McGraw-Hill, 1972, pp. 22-23.

Boiarsky, Carolyn. "The Relationship Between Cultural and Rhetorical Conventions: Engaging in International Communication." *Technical Communication Quarterly,* 4 (1995): 245-259.

Bokor, Gabe. "Teletranslating—Electronic File Transfer via Domestic and International Data Communications." *Technical Communication,* 37, no. 3 (1990): 292-295.

Bond, Michael H., Kwok Leung, and Kwok Choi Wang. "How Does Cultural Collectivism Operate? The Impact of Task and Maintenance Contributions on Renewal Distributions." *Journal of Cross-Cultural Psychology,* 13, no. 2 (1982): 186-200.

Bonk, Robert. "Writing Technical Documents for the Global Pharmaceutical Industry." *Technical Communication,* 46, no. 1 (1999): 98-106.

Bosley, Deborah S. "Cross-Cultural Collaboration: Whose Culture Is It Anyway?" *Technical Communication Quarterly,* 2, no. 1 (1993): 51-62.

Bosley, Deborah S. "Cross-Cultural Communication and Teamwork." *Global Talk* (Newsletter of the International Technical Communications Professional Interest Group of the Society for Technical Communication), 2, no. 3 (1994): 7-9.

Bowman, Joel P., and Tsugihiro Okuda. "Japanese-American Communication: Mysteries, Enigmas, and Possibilities." *The Bulletin of ABC,* 48 (1985): 18-21.

Bragg, Ed. "How Far Does English Reach?" *FORUM 85: PostHarvest* (1985): 9-16.

Brown, Rupert and Samuel Gaertner, eds. *Intergroup Processes.* Oxford: Blackwell, 2001.

Burton, Robert G. "The Human Awareness of Time: An Analysis." *Philosophy and Phenomenological Research,* 36, no. 3 (1976): 303-318.

Carnary, Daniel J., and Mariane Dainton. *Maintaining Relationships Through Communication: Relational, Contextual, and Cultural Variations.* Mahwah, NJ: Lawrence Erlbaum Associates, 2003.

Carrell, Patricia L., and Beverly H. Konneker. "Politeness: Comparing Native and Nonnative Judgments." *Language Learning,* 31, no. 1 (1981): 17-30.

Carroll, Ramonde. *Cultural Misunderstandings: The French-American Experience,* trans. Carolyn Volk. Chicago: University of Chicago Press, 1990.

Casady, Mona and Lynn Wasson. "Written Communication Skills of International Business Persons." *The Bulletin of ABC,* 57, no. 4 (1994): 36-40.

Casmir, F. L. "Third-Culture Building: A Paradigm Shift for International and Intercultural Communication." *Communication Yearbook,* no. 16, Newbury Park, CA: Sage, 1993, pp. 407-457.

Christians, Clifford G., and Michael Traber. *Communication Ethics and Universal Values.* Thousand Oaks, CA.: Sage Publications, 1997.

Chu, Steve. "Using Chopsticks and a Fork Together: Challenges and Strategies of Developing a Chinese/English Bilingual Web Site." *Technical Communication,* 46, no. 2 (1999): 206-219.

Clyne, Michael G. "Linguistics and Written Discourse in Particular Languages: Contrastive Studies of English and German." *Annual Review of Applied Linguistics,* 3 (1983): 85-98.

Condon, J. C. *Good Neighbors: Communicating with the Mexicans.* Yarmouth, ME: Intercultural Press, 1985.

Condon, J. C. *With Respect to the Japanese: A Guide for Americans.* Yarmouth, ME: Intercultural Press, 1984.

Condon, J. C., and F. Yousef. *An Introduction to Intercultural Communication.* New York: Macmillan, 1985.

Connor, Ulla and Robert B. Kaplan, eds. *Writing Across Languages: Analysis of L2 Text.* Reading, MA: Addison-Wesley, 1987.

Constantinides, Helen, et al. "Organizational and Intercultural Communication: An Annotated Bibliography." *Technical Communication Quarterly,* 10, no. 1 (2001): 31-59.

Copeland, Lennie and Lewis Griggs. *Going International: How to Make Friends and Deal Effectively in the Global Marketplace.* New York: Random House, 1985.

Coward, Nancy Caswell. "Cross-Cultural Communication: Is It Greek to You?" *Technical Communication,* 39, no. 2 (1992): 264-266.

Crismore, Avon, Raija Markkanen, and Margaret S. Steffensen. "Metadiscourse in Persuasive Writing: A Study of Texts Written by American and Finnish University Students." *Written Communication,* 10, no. 1 (1993): 39-71.

deGaldo, Elisa. "A European Evaluation of Three Document Formats for Hardware Installation Guides." In *Designing User Interfaces for International Use,* ed. Jakob Nielsen. New York: Elsevier, 1990, pp. 45-69.

deGaldo, Elisa. "Internationalization and Translation: Some Guidelines for the Design of Human-Computer Interfaces." In *Designing User Interfaces for International Use,* ed. Jakob Nielsen. New York: Elsevier, 1990, pp. 1-10.

Delori, Hatsi. "Centralizing Internationalization and Localization at Unisys Corporation." *Global Talk,* 3 (Fall 1994): 1.

deMente, Boye. *Chinese Etiquette and Ethics in Business,* 2nd ed. Lincolnwood, IL: NTC Business Books, 1994.

deMente, Boye. *How to Do Business with the Japanese: A Complete Guide to Customs and Business Practices.* Lincolnwood, IL: NTC Business Books, 1987.

deMente, Boye. *The Japanese Way of Doing Business: The Psychology of Management in Japan.* Englewood Cliffs, NJ: Prentice-Hall, 1981.

deMente, Boye. *Korean Etiquette and Ethics in Business,* 2nd ed. Lincolnwood, IL: NTC Business Books, 1994.

Demeter, Gusztay. "Misunderstandings Caused by Cross-Cultural Differences." *B. A. S.: British and American Studies,* 9, (2003): 205-210.

Dennett, Joann Temple. "Not to Say is Better than to Say: How Rhetorical Structure Reflects Cultural Context in Japanese-English Technical Writing." *IEEE Transactions on Professional Communication,* PC-31, no. 3 (1988): 116-119.

d'Épinay, Christine Lalive. "Time, Space and Socio-Cultural Identity: The Ethos of the Proletariat, Small Owners and Peasantry in an Aged Population." *International Social Science Journal,* 38, no. 1 (1986): 89-104.

Deutsch, Joseph. "Copyright Protection When Communicating to the World." *IEEE International Professional Communication Conference* (1989): 281-286.

DeVries, Mary. A. *Internationally Yours: Writing and Communicating in Today's Global Marketplace.* Boston: Houghton Mifflin, 1994.

Doob, Leonard William. *Patterning of Time.* New Haven: Yale University Press, 1971.

Dozier, Janelle Brinker, et al. "Need for Approval in Low-context and High-context Cultures: A Communications Approach to Cross-cultural Ethics." *Teaching Business Ethics,* 2, no. 2 (1998): 111-125.

Dragga, Sam. "Ethical Intercultural Technical Communication: Looking Through the Lens of Confucian Ethics." *Technical Communication Quarterly,* 8, no. 4 (1999): 365-381.

Driskill, Linda and Peggy Shaw. "Finding Intercultural Business Communication Research Cites in Companies." *The Bulletin of ABC,* 57, no. 3 (1994): 37-39.

Eiler, M. A., and D. Victor. "Genre and Function in the Italian and U.S. Business Letter." In *Proceedings of the Sixth Annual Conference on Languages and Communication for World Business and the Professions.* Ann Arbor, MI, 1988.

Ekström-Haasted, Marianne. "What to Do to Make a Manual Work in Different Markets." *FORUM 90: PostHarvest* (1990): 18-19.

Engholm, Christopher. *When Business East Meets Business West: The Guide to Practice and Protocol in the Pacific Rim.* New York: John Wiley & Sons, 1991.

Fang, Sheng-Ping, Ovid J. L. Tzeng, and Liz Alva. "Intralanguage vs. Interlanguage Stroop Effects in Two Types of Writing Systems." *Memory and Cognition,* 9, no. 6 (1981): 609-617.

Farinelli, Jean L. "Communicating Globally." *Enterprise* (January 1994): 47.

Feig, John P. *A Common Core: Thais and North Americans.* Revised by Elizabeth Mortlock. Yarmouth, ME: Interculture Press, 1989.

Feig, John P., and Lenore C. Yaffee. *Adjusting to the U.S.A.* Washington, DC: Washington International Center of Meridian House International, [no date].

Ferraro, Gary P. *The Cultural Dimensions of International Business.* Englewood Cliffs, NJ: Prentice-Hall, 1990.

Filipcová, Blanka and Jindich Filipee. "Society and Concepts of Time." *International Social Science Journal,* 38, no. 1 (1986): 19-32.

Fine, Marlene G. "New Voices in the Workplace: Research Directions in Multicultural Communication." *The Journal of Business Communication,* 28, no. 3 (1991): 259-275.

Fine, Margaret, Fern L. Johnson, and M. Sallyann Ryan. "Cultural Diversity in the Workplace." *Public Personnel Management,* 19, no. 3 (1990): 305-319.

Fisher, Glen. *Mindsets: The Role of Culture and Perception in International Relations* (2nd ed.) Yarmouth, ME: Intercultural Press, 1997.

Fitzgerald, Helen. *How Different Are We?: Spoken Discourse in Intercultural Communication: The Significance of the Situational Context.* Buffalo, NY: Multilingual Matters, 2003.

Fitzgerald, Tracy. "Translating EC Directives: What They Could Mean to You." *Communicator* [ISTC], ns 4, no. 2 (1993): 6-7.

Flint, Patricia, et al. "Going Online: Helping Technical Communicators Help Translators." *Technical Communication,* 46, no. 2 (1999): 238-248.

Fraser, J. T. *Time: The Familiar Stranger.* Amherst, MA: The University of Massachusetts Press, 1987.

Frost, P. J., et al., eds. *Organizational Culture.* Beverley Hills, CA: Sage, 1985.

Gatenby, Bev, and Margaret C. McLaren. "Teaching International Topics in the Business Communication Course: A Survey of ABC Members Beyond the United States." *The Bulletin of ABC,* 56, no. 4 (1993): 10-15.

Geertz, Clifford. *The Interpretation of Cultures: Selected Essays.* New York: Basic Books, 2000.

Geertz, Clifford. *Local Knowledge: Further Essays in Interpretive Anthropology.* New York: Basic Books, 1983.

Geng, Cui, et al. "Cross-Cultural Adaptation and Ethnic Communication: Two Structural Equation Models." *Howard Journal of Communications,* 9, no. 1 (1998): 69-72.

Gher, Leo A., and Hussein Y. Amin. *Civic Discourse and Digital Age Communications in the Middle East.* Stanford, CT: Ablex Publication Corp., 2000.

Gilleard, Jenni and John D. Gilleard. "Developing Cross-cultural Communication Skills." *Journal of Professional Issues in Engineering Education & Practice,* 128, no. 4 (2002): 187-191.

Goffman, Erving. *Frame Analysis: An Essay on the Organization of Experience.* New York: Harper and Row, 1974.

Goman, Carol Kinsy. "Cross-Cultural Business Practices." *Communication World,* 19, no. 2 (2002): 22-26.

Graham, John L. "The Influence of Culture on the Process of Business Negotiations: An Exploratory Study." *Journal of International Business Studies,* 16, no. 1 (1985): 81-96.

Grove, Laurel K. "Sign of the Times: Graphics for International Audiences." *IEEE International Professional Conference* (1989): 137-141.

Gudykunst, William B., L. P. Stewart, and S. Ting-Toomey, eds. *Communications, Culture, and Organizational Processes.* Beverly Hills, CA: Sage, 1985.

Gudykunst, William B. *Cross-Cultural and Intercultural Communication.* Thousand Oaks, CA: Sage Publications, 2003.

The GUI Guide: International Terminology for Windows Interface. Redmond, WA: Microsoft Press, 1993.

Guide to Macintosh Software Localization. Reading, MA: Addison-Wesley, 1992.

Gumperz, John. *Discourse Strategies.* Cambridge: Cambridge University Press, 1982.

Haas, Christina and Jeffrey L. Funk. "Shared Information: Some Observations of Communication in Japanese Technical Setting." *Technical Communication,* 36, no. 4 (1989): 362-367.

Hager, Peter J., and Scheiber, H. J., eds. *Managing Global Communication in Science and Technology*. New York: Wiley, 2000.

Hall, Edward T. *Beyond Culture*. New York: Anchor Press, 1989.

Hall, Edward T. *The Dance of Life: The Other Dimension of Time*. Garden City, NY: Anchor Press/Doubleday, 1983.

Hall, Edward T. *The Hidden Dimension*. Garden City, NY: Anchor, 1996.

Hall, Edward T. *The Silent Language*. Garden City, NY: Doubleday, 1959.

Hall, Edward T., and Mildred Reed Hall. *Hidden Differences: Doing Business with the Japanese*. Garden City, NY: Anchor Press/Doubleday, 1987.

Hall, Edward T., and Mildred Reed Hall. *Understanding Cultural Differences*. Yarmouth, ME: Intercultural Press, 1990.

Hallman, Mark I. "Differentiating Technical Translation from Technical Writing." *Technical Communication*, 37, no. 3 (1990): 244-247.

Halpern, Jeanne W. "Business Communication in China: A Second Perspective." *The Journal of Business Communication*, 20, no. 4 (1983): 43-55.

Hancock, Ian, and Loretto Todd. *International English Usage*. New York: New York University Press, 1987.

Haneda, Saburo and Hirosuke Shima. "Japanese Communication Behavior as Reflected in Letter Writing." *The Journal of Business Communication*, 19, no. 1 (1982): 19-32.

Harcourt, J. "A New Cross-Cultural Course: Communicating in the International Business Environment." *The Bulletin of the ABC*, 51, no. 3 (1988): 11-13.

Harms, L. S. *Intercultural Communication*. New York: Harper & Row, 1973.

Harris, Philip R., Sarah Moran, and Robert T. Morgan. *Managing Cultural Differences: Global Leadership Strategies for the Twenty-First Century*, 6th ed. New York: Elsevier, 2004.

Harrison, P. A. *Behaving Brazilian: A Comparison of Brazilian and North American Social Behavior*. Cambridge, MA: Newbury House, 1983.

Hartman, R. R. K. *Contrastive Textology: Comparative Discourse Analysis in Applied Linguistics*. Heidelberg: Julius Gross Verlag, 1980.

Haworth, Dwight A., and Grant T. Savage. "A Channel-Ratio Model of Intercultural Communication." *Journal of Business Communication*, 26, no. 3 (1989): 231-254.

Hein, Robert G. "Culture and Communication." *Technical Communication*, 38, no. 1 (1991): 125-126.

Higgins, Richard B. *The Search for Corporate Strategic Credibility: Concepts and Cases in Global Strategy Communications*. Westport, CT: Quorum Books, 1996.

Hofstede, Geert. "Cultural Predictors of National Negotiation Styles." In *Processes of International Negotiation*, ed. Frances Mautner-Markof. Boulder, CO: Westview Press, 1989, pp. 193-201.

Hofstede, Geert. *Culture's Consequences: Comparing Values, Behaviors, Institutions, and Organizations Across Nations*, 2nd ed. Thousand Oaks, CA: Sage, 2001.

Hofstede, Geert. *Cultures and Organizations: Software of the Mind.* New York: McGraw-Hill Book Company, 1991.

Hoft, Nancy L. *International Technical Communication: How to Export Information about High Technology.* New York: John Wiley & Sons, 1995.

Hoft, Nancy L. "Preparing for the Inevitable: Localizing Computer Documentation." *SIGDOC '91 Conference Proceedings,* (1991): 37.

Hoft, Nancy L., ed. "Global Issues, Local Concerns" (special issue). *Technical Communication,* 46, no. 2 (1999): 132-290.

Hooker, John. *Working Across Cultures.* Stanford, CA: Stanford Business Books, 2003.

Hoopes, D. S., ed. *Readings in Intercultural Communication,* vol. 1. Pittsburgh: Intercultural Communications Network, 1975.

Hudson, Glenda A. "Internationalizing Technical Communication Courses." In *Studies in Technical Communication: Proceedings of the 1990 CCCC and NCTE Meetings.* Denton, TX: North Texas University Press, 1990, pp. 135-145.

Hymes, Dell. *Foundations in Sociolinguistics: An Ethnographic Approach.* Philadelphia: University of Pennsylvania Press, 1974.

Jablin, Frederick M., and Linda L. Putnam, eds. *The New Handbook of Organizational Communication.* Thousand Oaks, CA: Sage, 2001.

Jameson, Daphne A. "Strategies for Overcoming Barriers Inherent in Cross-Cultural Research." *Bulletin of ABC,* 57, no. 3 (1994): 39-40.

Jameson, Daphne A. "Using a Simulation to Teach Intercultural Communication in Business Communication Courses." *Bulletin of ABC,* 56, no. 1 (1993): 3-11.

Jandt, Fred E. *Intercultural Communication: An Introduction,* 3rd ed. Thousand Oaks, CA: Sage Publications, 1998.

Jandt, Fred E., and Dolores Tanno. "Decoding Domination, Encoding Self-Determination: Intercultural Communication Research Processes." *Howard Journal of Communications,* 12, no. 3 (2001): 119-135.

Jingjuan, Yu. "How to Deliver a Successful Lecture in China." *IEEE Transactions on Professional Communication,* PC-29, no. 2 (1986): 19-22.

Johnston, Jean. "Business Communication in Japan." *Journal of Business Communication,* 17 (1984): 65-70.

Jones, Scott, et al. *Developing International User Information.* Bedford, MA: Digital Press, 1992.

Kakar, S. "Authority Patterns and Subordinate Behavior in Indian Organizations." *Administrative Science Quarterly,* 16, no. 3 (1971): 298-301.

Kaplan, Robert B. "Contrastive Rhetoric and Second Language Learning: Notes Toward a Theory of Contrastive Rhetoric." In *Writing Across Languages: Analysis of L2 Text,* ed. Ulla Connor and Robert B. Kaplan. Reading, MA: Addison-Wesley, 1987, pp. 275-304.

Kaplan, Robert B. "Cultural Thought Patterns in Inter-Cultural Education." In *Readings on English as a Second Language: For Teachers and Teacher-Trainees,* ed. Kenneth Croft. Cambridge, MA: Winthrop Publishers,

1972, pp. 245-262. (Previously published in *Language Learning,* 16 (1966): 1-20.

Kaplan, Robert B. "Cultural Thought Patterns in Inter-Cultural Education." In *Readers on English as a Second Language for Teachers and Teacher Trainees,* 2nd ed., ed. Kenneth Croft. Boston: Little, Brown and Company, 1980, pp. 399-418.

Katan, David. *Translating Cultures: An Introduction for Translators, Interpreters, and Mediators.* Northampton, MA: St. Jerome Pub., 2003.

Kato, Hiroki and Joan S. Kato. *Understanding and Working with the Japanese Business World.* Englewood Cliffs, NJ: Prentice Hall, 1992.

Kelley, Lane and R. Worthley. "The Role of Culture in Comparative Management: A Cross-Cultural Perspective." *Academy of Management Journal,* 24, no. 1 (1981): 164-173.

Kenelly, Cynthia Hartman. *The Digital Guide to Developing International Software.* Bedford, MA: Digital Press, 1991.

Kennedy, George A. *Comparative Rhetoric: An Historical and Cross-Cultural Introduction.* New York: Oxford University Press, 1998.

Kenna, Peggy and Sondra Lacy. *Business Japan: A Practical Guide to Understanding Japanese Business.* Lincolnwood, IL: NTC Business Books, 1994.

Kenna, Peggy and Sondra Lacy. *Business China: A Practical Guide to Understanding Chinese Business.* Lincolnwood, IL: NTC Business Books, 1994.

Kenna, Peggy and Sondra Lacy. *Business France: A Practical Guide to Understanding French Business.* Lincolnwood, IL: NTC Business Books, 1994.

Kenna, Peggy and Sondra Lacy. *Business Germany: A Practical Guide to Understanding German Business.* Lincolnwood, IL: NTC Business Books, 1994.

Kenna, Peggy and Sondra Lacy. *Business Italy: A Practical Guide to Understanding Italian Business.* Lincolnwood, IL: Passport Books, 1995.

Kenna, Peggy, and Sondra Lacy. *Business Mexico: A Practical Guide to Understanding Mexican Business.* Lincolnwood, IL: NTC Business Books, 1994.

Killingsworth, M. Jimmie and Michael K. Gilbertson. *Signs, Genres, and Communities in Technical Communication.* Amityville, NY: Baywood, 1992.

Kilpatrick, Retha H. "International Business Communication Practices." *Journal of Business Communication,* 21, no. 4 (1984): 33-44.

Kim, Young Kim. *Becoming Intercultural: An Integrating Theory of Communication and Cross-Cultural Adaptation.* Thousand Oaks, CA: Sage Publications, 2001.

Kinosita, Koreo. "Language Habits of the Japanese." *The Bulletin of ABC,* 51 (1988): 35-40.

Kirkman, John. "Choosing Language for Effective Technical Writing." In *ISTC Handbook for Technical Writing and Publication Techniques,* ed. Mike Austin. London: ISTC, 1990, pp. 1-28.

Kirkman, John, Christine Snow, and Ian Watson. "Controlled English as an Alternative to Multiple Translation." *IEEE Transactions on Professional Communication,* PC-21, no. 4 (1978): 159-161.

Klein, Fred. "A Multilingual Market: Exporting to Europe." *Technical Communication,* 36, no. 2 (1989): 159-161.

Klein, Fred, ed. "International Technical Communication." *Technical Communication,* column appearing irregularly, written by guest writers.

Kohl, John R., et al. "The Impact of Language and Culture on Technical Communication in Japan." *Technical Communication,* 40, no. 1 (1993): 62-73.

Kostelnick, Charles. Cultural Adaptation and Information Design: Two Contrasting Views. *IEEE Transactions on Professional Communication,* PC-38, no. 4 (1995): 182-196.

Kras, E. S. *Management in Two Cultures: Bridging the Gap between U.S. and Mexican Managers.* Yarmouth, ME: Intercultural Press, 1989.

Kroeber, A. L., and C. Kluckholn. *Culture: A Critical Review of Concepts and Definitions.* New York: Vintage, 1963.

Kumon, Shumpei. "Some Principles Governing the Thought and Behavior of Japan (Contextualists)." *Journal of Japanese Studies,* 8 (1984): 5-28.

Landis, Dan, ed. *Handbook of Intercultural Training: Issues in Theory and Design,* 3rd ed. Thousand Oaks, CA: Sage, 2004.

Laroche, Lionel. *Managing Cultural Diversity in Technical Professions.* Boston: Butterworth-Heinemann, 2003.

Latham, M. Gerald. "Internationalization of Business Communication." *Mid-South Business Journal,* 2 (1982): 16-18.

Leppert, Paul A. *Doing Business with the Koreans: A Handbook for Executives.* Chula Vista, CA: Patton Pacific Press, 1987.

Leppet, Paul A. *Doing Business with Singapore: A Handbook for Executives.* Chula Vista, CA: Patton Pacific Press, 1990.

Li, Jenny. *Passport China: Your Pocket Guide to Chinese Business, Customs and Etiquette.* Novato, CA: World Trade Press, 1996.

Lie, Rico. *Spaces of Intercultural Communication: An Interdisciplinary Introduction to Communication, Culture, and Globalizing/Localizing Identities.* Creskill, NJ: Hampton Press, 2003.

Limaye, Mohan R., and David R. Victor. "Cross-Cultural Business Communication Research: State of the Art and Hypotheses for the 1990s." *Journal of Business Communication,* 28, no. 3 (1991): 277-299.

Lipson, Carol S. "The Effects of Culture on Prose Handling: Preparing for an Influx of Foreign Students in Technical Writing Courses." *Technical Writing Teacher,* 10, no. 2/3 (1983): 230-241.

Lipson, Carol S. "Preparing for the Influx of Foreign Students in Technical Courses: Understanding Their Backgrounds." In *Technical Communication: Perspectives for the Eighties,* comp. J. C. Mathes and T. E. Pinelli. Langley, VA: NASA Conference Publication, Part I, 1981, pp. 173-179.

Littlejohn, Stephen W., and Karen A. Foss. *Theories of Human Communication,* 8th ed. Belmont, CA: Wadsworth, 2005.

Localization for Japan, Cupertino, CA: Apple Computer Company, 1992.

Lovitt, Carl and Dixie Goswami, eds. *Exploring the Rhetoric of International Professional Communication: An Agenda for Teachers and Researchers.* Amityville, NY: Baywood Publishing, 1999.

Luce, Louise Fiber and Elise C. Smith, eds. *Toward Internationalism: Readings in Cross-cultural Communication,* 2nd ed. Cambridge: Newbury House, 1987.

Lunde, Ken. *Understanding Japanese Information Processing.* Sebastopol, CA: O'Reilley & Associates, 1993.

Lüscher, M. (Several works in German.) Basel: Test-Verlag, 1948-1961.

Mackin, John. "Surmounting the Barrier Between Japanese and English Technical Documents." *Technical Communication,* 36, no. 4 (1989): 346-351.

Maines, David R. "Culture and Temporality." *Cultural Dynamics,* 2, no. 1 (1984): 107-123.

Marquardt, Michael J., and Lisa Horvath. *Global Teams: How Top Multinationals Span Boundaries and Cultures with High-Speed Teamwork.* Palo Alto, CA: Davies-Black Publication, 2001.

Matsui, Kyoko. "Document Design from a Japanese Perspective: Improving the Relationship Between Clients and Writers." *Technical Communication,* 36, no. 4 (1989): 341-345.

McCaffrey, James A., and Craig R. Hafner. "When Two Cultures Collide: Doing Business Overseas." *Training and Development Journal,* 39, no. 10 (1985): 26-31.

McCain, Barbara and Mary Khalili. *Transitions, a Guide to Understanding Intercultural Business Communications,* rev. ed. Houston, TX: Dame Publications, 1999.

McDonald, John W. "Communicating Across Barriers at Home and Abroad." *FORUM 85: PostHarvest* (1985): 80-85.

McGrath, Joseph E., ed. *The Social Psychology of Time: New Perspectives.* Newbury Park, CA: Sage Publications, 1988. (Contains James M. Jones, "Cultural Differences in Temporal Perspectives: Instrumental and Expressive Behaviors in Time"; Robert V. Levine, "The Pace of Life Across Cultures"; Rebecca Warner, "Rhythm in Social Interaction"; Janice R. Kelley, "Entrainment in Individual and Group Behavior"; Jonathan L. Freedman and Donald R. Edwards, "Time Pressure, Task Performance, and Enjoyment"; John P. Robinson, "Time-Diary Evidence About the Social Psychology of Everyday Life"; Richard L. Moreland and John M. Levine, "Group Dynamics Over Time: Development and Socialization of Small Groups"; Allan W. Wicker and Jeanne C. King, "Life Cycles of Behavior Settings"; Carol M. Werner, Lois M. Haggard, Irwin Altman, and Diana Oxley, "Temporal Qualities of Rituals and Celebrations: A Comparison of Christmas Street and Zuni Shalako"; and Daniel Stokols, "Transformational Processes in People-Environment Relations.")

Mealing, David. "The Exporter's Guide to the Galaxy." *Communicator* [ISTC], ns 4, no. 2 (1993): 2-5.

Miller, Debra A. *Multicultural Communications: A Bibliography.* New York: PRSA Foundation, 1993.

Mirshafiei, Moshen. "Culture as an Element in Teaching Technical Writing." *1992 Proceedings of the Annual Conference.* Arlington,. VA: Society for Technical Communication, 1992, pp. 557-560. (See also *Technical Communication,* 41, no. 2 (1994): 276-282, for an expanded version.)

Moder, Carol and Martinovic-Zic, Aida. *Discourse Across Languages and Cultures.* Philadelphia, PA: John Benjamin Publication, 2004.

Mody, Bella, ed. *Handbook of International and Intercultural Communications,* 2nd ed. Thousand Oaks, CA: Sage Publications, 2003.

Mole, John. *When in Rome . . . : A Business Guide to Cultures and Customs in 12 European Nations.* New York: American Management Association, 1990.

Mollov, Ben and Chiam Lavie. "Culture, Dialogue, and Perception Change in the Israeli-Palestinian Conflict." *International Journal of Conflict Management,* 12, no. 1, (2001): 69-87.

Monaco, Jill. "Adventures in Localization: How to Adapt Your Product to Different Audiences." *1991 Proceedings of the Annual Conference.* Arlington, VA: Society for Technical Communication, 1991, pp. RT-35–RT-36.

Mulac, Anthony. "Empirical Support for the Gender-as-Culture Hypothesis. An Intercultural Analysis of Male/Female Language Differences." *Human Communication Research,* 27, no. 1 (2001): 121-152.

Murray, Melba Jerry and Hugh Hay-Roe. "International Scientific and Technical Writing." In *Engineered Writing,* 2nd ed. Tulsa, OK: PennWell Books, 1986, pp. 207-233.

Musambira, George W. "A Comparison of Modernist and Postmodernist Accounts of Cross-Cultural Communication Between African Societies and the United States." *Howard Journal of Communications,* 11, no. 2 (2000): 145-162.

Nash, Gail. "Cross-Cultural Communication and Technical Communication." *1990 Proceedings of the International Technical Communication Conference.* Arlington, VA: Society for Technical Communication, 1990, pp. ET-188–ET-190.

Neuliep, James William. *Intercultural Communication: A Contextual Approach,* 2nd ed. Boston: Houghton Mifflin, 2002.

Nielsen, Jakob. *Designing User Interfaces for International Use.* New York: Elsevier, 1990.

Nishishiba, Masami and L. David Ritchie. "The Concept of Trustworthiness: A Cross-Cultural Comparison Between Japanese and U.S. Business People." *Journal of Applied Communication Research,* 28, no. 4 (2000): 347-368.

Nydell, Margaret. *Understanding Arabs: A Guide for Westerners.* Yarmouth, ME: Interculture Press, 1987.

Oetzel, J. *Managing Intercultural Conflicts Effectively.* Thousand Oaks, CA: Sage Publications, 2001.

Oetzel, John, et al. "Face and Facework in Conflict: A Cross-Cultural Comparison of China, Germany, Japan, and the United States." *Communication Monographs,* 68, no. 3 (2001): 235-258.

Ojwang, Humphrey J. "Interactive Aspects of Functional Literacy and the Socio-Cultural Environment." *FORUM 90 PostHarvest* (1990): 45-50.

O'Rourke, James S., IV. "Intercultural Business Communication: Building a Course from the Ground Up." *The Bulletin of ABC,* 56, no. 4 (1993): 22-27.

Osgood, Charles E., William H. May, and Murray S. Miron. *Cross Cultural Universals of Affective Meaning.* Urbana: University of Illinois Press, 1975

Osigweh, C. A. B., ed. *Organizational Science Abroad: Constraints and Perspectives.* New York: Plenum Press, 1989.

O'Sullivan, Siegrum. "Writing Documentation with Translation in Mind." *TECDOC 92* (1992): 21-25.

Parkin, Ernest J., Jr. "Teaching Technical Writing to Non-Native Speakers of English." *Journal of Technical Writing and Communication,* 13, no. 1 (1983): 1-6.

Patrushev, V. D. "Past and Future Changes in Soviet Workers' Time-Budget." *International Social Science Journal,* 38, no. 1 (1986): 77-88.

Peng, Shiyong. *Culture and Conflict Management in Foreign-Invested Enterprises in China: An Intercultural Communication Perspective.* New York: Peter Lang, 2003.

Peterson, David A. T. "Addressing Nonnative Readers." In *Scientific and Technical Writing: A Manual of Style,* ed. Philip Rubens. New York: Henry Holt, 1992, pp. 213-238.

Phillips, WandaJane. *Creating Texts for an International Audience: 2 Important Issues.* Ottawa, Ontario: International Development Research Centre, 1993. (Handout at the 40th Annual STC Conference, Dallas, TX, 1993.)

Potvin, Janet H., and Robert L. Woods. "Technical Communication and the Nonnative Speaker." *Engineering Education,* 74, no. 3 (1983): 171-173.

Pronovost, Gilles. "Introduction: Time in a Sociological and Historical Perspective." *International Social Science Journal,* 38, no. 1 (1986): 5-18.

Purves, Alan C. *Writing Across Languages and Cultures: Issues in Contrastive Rhetoric.* Newbury Park: Sage, 1988.

Qiuye, Wang. "A Cross-Cultural Comparison of the Use of Graphics in Scientific and Technical Communication." *Technical Communication,* 47, no. 4 (2000): 553-560.

Randlesome, Collin and William Brierley. *Business Cultures in Europe.* Boston, MA: Butterworth-Heinenmann, 1993.

Rezsohazy, Rudolf. "Recent Social Developments and Changes in Attitudes to Time." *International Social Science Journal,* 38, no. 1 (1986): 33-48.

Ricks, David A. *Blunders in International Business,* 3rd ed. Malden, MA: Blackwell, 1999.

Riggs, Brian. "Overcoming Cultural Differences." *Presentations* (October 1994): 10, 14.

Rodgers, Drew. *Business Communications: International Case Studies in English.* Cambridge: Cambridge University Press, 1998.

Ronen, Simdia, and Oded Shenkar. "Clustering Countries on Attitudinal Dimensions: A Review and Synthesis." *Academy of Management Review,* 10 (1985): 435-454.

Rosseel, Peter and Mary K. Roll. "Cross-Cultural Technical Translations: From an Isolated Translator to a Business Communicator." *1990 Proceedings of the International Technical Communication Conference.* Arlington, VA: Society for Technical Communication, 1990, pp. RT-99–RT-102.

Rowland, Diana. *Japanese Business Etiquette: A Practical Guide to Success with the Japanese,* 2nd ed. New York: Warner Books, 1993.

Rubel, Paula and Abraham Rosman, eds. *Translating Cultures: Perspectives on Translation and Anthropology.* Oxford, NY: Berg, 2003.

Samuel, Nicole. "Free Time in France: A Historical and Sociological Survey." *International Social Science Journal,* 38, no. 1 (1986): 49-63.

Saphiere, Dianne H. "Online Cross-Cultural Collaboration." *Training and Development,* 54, no. 10 (2000): 71-73.

Sapir, Edward. *Culture, Language and Personality.* Los Angeles, 1964.

Savignon, Sandra J., and Pavel Sysoyev. "Sociocultural Strategies for a Dialogue of Cultures." *Modern Language Journal,* 86, no. 4 (2002): 508-524.

Schiller, H. I. *Communication and Cultural Domination.* New York: Knopf, 1978.

Schnell, James. *Case Studies in Culture and Communication: A Group Perspective.* Lanham, MD: Lexington Books, 2003.

Schultz, S. et al. *The Digital Technical Documentation Handbook.* Burlington, MA: Digital Press, 1993.

Scollon, Ron and Suzanne Wong Scollon. *Intercultural Communication: A Discourse Approach,* 2nd ed. Oxford: Basil Blackwell, 1995.

Scott, James Calvert. "Teaching an International Business Communication Course." *The Bulletin of ABC,* 57, no. 1 (1994): 44-45.

Seligman, Scott D. *Dealing with the Chinese: A Practical Guide to Business Etiquette in the People's Republic Today.* New York: Warner Books, 1989.

Shi-Xu. "Critical Pedagogy and Intercultural Communication: Creating Discourses of Diversity, Equality, Common Goals and Rational-Moral Motivation." *Journal of Intercultural Studies,* 22, no. 3 (2001): 279-293.

Sims, Brenda R., and Stephen A. Guice. "Explaining the Difficulties of International Business Letters: Readability, Grammaticality, and Cultural Sensitivity." In *Studies in Technical Communication: Proceedings of the 1990 CCCC and NCTE Meetings,* ed. Brenda R. Sims. Denton, TX: University of North Texas, 1990, pp. 147-162.

Singer, Marshall R. *Perception and Identity in Intercultural Communication.* Yarmouth, ME: Intercultural Press, 1998.

Smithies, Michael. "Formal Style in an Oral Culture: Problems at the University Level." *ELT,* 35, no. 4 (1981): 369-372.

Spencer, Kathy and Peggy Yates. "Tell it to the World: Technical Communication in the Global Marketplace." *1990 Proceedings of the International Technical Communication Conference.* Arlington, VA: Society for Technical Communication, 1990, pp. RT-149–RT-152.

St. Amant, Kirk. "Considering China: A Perspective for Technical Communicators." *Technical Communication,* 48, no. 4 (2001): 385-388.

Stevenson, Dwight W. "Audience Analysis Across Cultures." *Journal of Technical Writing and Communication,* 13 (1983): 319-330.

Subbiah, Mahalingam. "Adding a New Dimension to the Teaching of Audience Analysis: Cultural Awareness." *IEEE Transactions on Professional Communication,* 35 (1992): 14-18.

Sukaviriya, Piyawadee and Lucy Moran. "User Interface for Asia." In *Designing User Interfaces for International Users,* ed. Jakob Nielsen. New York: Elsevier, 1990, pp. 189-218.

Sullivan, Jeremiah J., and Naoki Kameda. "The Concept of Profit and Japanese-American Business Communication Problem." *Journal of Business Communication,* 19, no. 1 (1982): 33-39.

Sullivan, Jeremiah and Sully Taylor. "A Cross-Cultural Test of Compliance-Gaining Theory." *Management Communication Quarterly,* 5, no. 2 (1991): 220-239.

Swales, John. "Discourse Communities, Genres, and English as an International Language." *World Englishes,* 7 (1988): 211-220.

Taylor, Dave. *Global Software: Developing Applications for the International Market.* New York: Springer-Verlag, 1992.

Tessman, Rota. "Results of a Survey and Discussion about Science Writing Style." *FORUM 85: PostHarvest* (1985): 28-38.

Thatcher, Barry. "Cultural and Rhetorical Adaptations for South American Audiences." *Technical Communication,* 46, no. 2 (1999): 177-195.

Thatcher, Barry. "Issues of Validity in Intercultural Professional Communication Research." *Journal of Business and Technical Communication,* 15, no. 4 (2001): 458-489.

Thomson, Ian. *The Documentation of the European Communities: A Guide.* London: Mansell Publishing, Ltd., 1995.

Thompson-Panos, Karyn and Maria Thomas-Ružić. "The Least You Should Know About Arabic: Implications for the ESL Writing Instructor." *TESOL Quarterly,* 17, no. 4 (1983): 609-623.

Thrush, Emily A. "Bridging the Gaps: Technical Communication in an International and Multicultural Society," *Technical Communication Quarterly*, 2, no. 3 (1993): 271-283.

Thrush, Emily A. "Plain English? A Study of Plain English Vocabulary and International Audiences." *Technical Communication*, 48, no. 3 (2001): 289-296.

Ting-Toomey, S. "Toward a Theory of Conflict and Culture." In *Communication, Culture, and Organizational Processes*, eds. W. B. Gudykunst, L. Stewart, and S. Ting-Toomey. Beverly Hills, CA: Sage, 1985.

Trompenaars, Fons. *Riding the Waves of Culture: Understanding Diversity in Global Business*. Burr Ridge, IL: Irwin, 1994.

Trompenaars, Fons and Charles Hampden-Turner. *The Seven Dimensions of Capitalism: Value Systems for Creating Wealth in the United States, Britain, Japan, Germany, France, Sweden, and The Netherlands*. London: Piartkus, 1993.

Tzeng, Ovid J. L., and William S.-Y. Wang. "The First Two R's." *American Scientist*, 71, no. 3 (1983): 238-243.

Ulijn, Jan M. "Is Cultural Rewriting of American Technical Documents Needed for the European Market? Some Experimental Evidence from French and Dutch Technical Documents." In *International Dimensions of Technical Communication*, ed. Deborah Andrews. Arlington, VA: Society for Technical Communication, 1995.

Ulijn, Jan M., Jeroen Hoppenbrouwers, and Gerke Mulder. "Writing for a Client in International Business and Technology: Does Culture Affect His/Her Expectations? Some Evidence from Reading Industrial Research Proposals and Technical Manuals." *IPCC92 Sante Fe Proceedings* (1992): IC6.3/573–IC6.3/578.

Ulijn, Jan M., and Kirk St.Amant. "Mutual Intercultural Perception: How Does It Affect Technical Communication? Some Data from China, the Netherlands, Germany, France, and Italy." *Technical Communication*, 47, no. 2 (2000): 220-237.

Ulijn, Jan M., and Judith B. Strother. *Communicating in Business and Technology: From Psycholinguistic Theory to International Practice*. Frankfurt/Berne: Peter Lang Publishing, 1995.

Uren, Emmanuel, Robert Howard, and Tiziana Perinotti. *An Introduction: Software Internationalization and Localization*. New York: Van Nostrand Reinhold, 1993.

Varner, Iris I. "A Comparison of American and French Business Correspondence." *Journal of Business Communication*, 25, no. 1 (1988): 55-65.

Victor, David A. "Advancing Research in International Business Communication." *The Bulletin of ABC*, 57, no. 3 (1994): 41-42.

Victor, David A. *International Business Communication*. New York: HarperCollins Publishers, 1992.

Victor, David A. "Franco-American Business Communication Practices: A Survey." *World Communication*, 16, no. 2 (1987): 157-175.

Walker, Danielle Medina, et al. *Doing Business Internationally: The Guide to Cross-Cultural Success,* 2nd ed. New York: McGraw-Hill, 2003.

Wang, Charlie. "Right Appeals for the 'Right Self': Connectedness-Separateness Self-Schema and Cross-cultural Persuasion." *Journal of Marketing Communications,* 6, no. 4 (2000): 205-217.

Wang, W. S.-Y. "The Chinese Language." *Scientific American,* 228 (1973): 50-60.

Ward, James. "Editing in a Bilingual, Bicultural Context." *Journal of Technical Writing and Communication,* 18, no. 3 (1988): 221-226.

Warren, Thomas L. "Increasing User Acceptance of Technical Information in Cross-Cultural Communication." *Journal of Technical Writing and Communication,* 34, no. 4 (2004): 249-264.

Warren, Thomas L. "Cultural Influences as Technical Manuals." *Journal of Technical Writing and Communication,* 32, no. 2 (2002): 111-123.

Warren, Thomas L. "Communicating Style Rules to Editors of International Standards: An Analysis of ISO TC 184/SC4 Style Documents." *Journal of Technical Writing and Communication,* 31, no. 2 (2001): 159-173.

Weiss, Edmond H. *The Elements of International English Style: A Guide to Writing Correspondence, Reports, Technical Documents, and Internet Pages for a Global Audience.* Armonk, NY: M. E. Sharpe, 2005.

Weiss, Timothy. "'The Gods Must Be Crazy': The Challenge of the Intercultural." *Journal of Business and Technical Communication,* 7, no. 2 (1993): 196-217.

Weymouth, L. C. "Establishing Quality Standards and Trade Regulations for Technical Writing in World Trade." *Technical Communication,* 37, no. 2 (1990): 143-147.

Wik, P. *How to Do Business with the People's Republic of China.* Reston, VA: Reston Publishing Company, 1984.

Wiles, Debbie. "Single Sourcing and Chinese Culture: A Perspective on Skills Development Within Western Organizations and the People's Republic of China." *Technical Communication,* 50, no. 3 (2003): 371-384.

Winters, Elaine. "Thoughts on Achieving International Technical Communication Success." *Intercom,* 40, no. 3 (1994): 7.

Zaharna, R. S. "Intercultural Communication and International Public Relations: Exploring Parallels." *Communication Quarterly,* 48, no. 1 (2000): 85-101.

Zong, Baolin and H. W. Hildebrant. "Business Communication in the People's Republic of China." *Journal of Business Communication,* 20, no. 1 (1983): 25-33.

Index

Other Books of Interest in Baywood's Technical Communications Series

Series Editor: Charles H. Sides